I0558129

Voice Training

A Comprehensive Guide to Voice Training

(A Comprehensive Guide to Voice Training and Accent Reduction)

Christopher Wells

Published By **Bella Frost**

Christopher Wells

All Rights Reserved

Voice Training: A Comprehensive Guide to Voice Training (A Comprehensive Guide to Voice Training and Accent Reduction)

ISBN 978-1-9995502-4-0

No part of this guidebook shall be reproduced in any form without permission in writing from the publisher except in the case of brief quotations embodied in critical articles or reviews.

Legal & Disclaimer

The information contained in this book is not designed to replace or take the place of any form of medicine or professional medical advice. The information in this book has been provided for educational & entertainment purposes only.

The information contained in this book has been compiled from sources deemed reliable, and it is accurate to the best of the Author's knowledge; however, the Author cannot guarantee its accuracy and validity and cannot be held liable for any errors or omissions. Changes are periodically made to this book. You must consult your doctor or get professional medical advice before using any of the suggested remedies, techniques, or information in this book.

Upon using the information contained in this book, you agree to hold harmless the Author from and against any damages, costs, and expenses, including any legal fees potentially resulting from the application of any of the information provided by this guide. This disclaimer applies to any damages or injury caused by the use and application, whether directly or indirectly, of any advice or information presented, whether for breach of contract, tort, negligence, personal injury, criminal intent, or under any other cause of action.

You agree to accept all risks of using the information presented inside this book. You need to consult a professional medical practitioner in order to ensure you are both able and healthy enough to participate in this program.

Table Of Contents

Chapter 1: Noise And Voice

Is there a difference between the two? One might then ask: What type of sound is it, and who's voice? In order to answer this question, it is essential to provide the anticipated difference. What is the reason for noises and voices? Is there something which could trigger a sound with no voice? This is a fascinating question which require answers to those with an interest in science. There are, of course, the sounds and voices of various sounds of objects made from material and living things throughout the universe.

The sound of an engine, crickets, of wind and of the water, rains, and the voices of God and angels along with equally demonic and satanic voices are the main distinction. An engine's sound is only detected when it is in excellent condition and moving. Similar to how a person's voice could show that he's alive through his words. We will once more look at the two aspects of sound creation in relation to vocal perception and noise.

The cause of noises is the voice, but they are created. If the cause of a noise by a sound, it can also be created. Similar to when there is a voice being produced or sounded, it can also be made. If someone is speaking without the proper pronunciation of his voice, certain people, they could make a sound. It is due to the fact that his voice isn't being heard. Therefore, some individuals are making noises believing they are talking or uttering a sound. This debate is to differentiate sounds from voices of an untrained person during the course. Every material that is produced will have its the form of a tone. So, for instance, iron sounds different to wood, and iron sounds different sounds different from rubber.

Guitar sounds produce an distinctive melody sound similar to the sound of an instrument like a flute or drum. It is also true for female and male voice in the majority of cases. While some men have tiny voices, just like females, it's also real that females possess a distinct quality to male voices as well. This is that it is important to distinguish the noise that a voice produces in this effective therapy for vocal training.

IS YOUR VOICE PLEASANT ENOUGH?

Does your voice sound pleasant enough that it is listened to by other?

This is a question to inspire or motivate you to your voice

treatment for grooming to ensure a great version of the vocal manipulation. "We want to hear you, not your voice," one person has told. Your voice, in fact, is the most important aspect of your personal identity. It's your phone number or trade name and your Personal Logo. It's also a way to advertise something, and, in this case, announces to the world exactly what type of person you are. Impersonating someone's voice is to steal his persona. "Actress Better Midler sued a major Automobile Corporation for imitating her voice in several of its commercial specifically her attorney noted and she won the case"

The news or article is taken from the book Essentials of Vocal and Articulation written from Lyle Mayer, the 11th edition.

YOUR VOICE IS LONELY YOURS

Do you think that your voice can't be and you are the only one who hears it wherever you travel? The only voice you have is yours that is yours around the globe, so it's exactly similar to your voice. Your individual length, breath the quality, and even its appearance. and both have a covered melody whether it is during speech or singing.

So your voice is that of you, both in the surface and through audio. Your voice is distinctive and distinctive that it is not able to attract others to be admired just only you. The voice may be a resemblance to someone else's tone of voice, but the tone isn't theirs but rather yours. You'll soon realize the person was actually you. Did you know that the legal courts now accept the voiceprint as proof accepted as a fingerprint to identify the person? While the majority of opera singers are adamant. Enrico Caruso, the world's most famous tenor was not? He used to smoke two packets of super-strong Egyptians cigarettes daily. The famous Emperor Nero's voice was so weak and rough that his senators chuckled at the senate. To enhance his voice performance, he would spend hours on his back, smacking a piece of lead slapped on his chest. This didn't work. In the book The Basics in Voice and Articulation written from Lyle Mayer.

What should one accomplish at the conclusion of this discussion? This is how one can recognize one's voice as well as its high quality production. In addition to &l, it is the thing people look at in all comments about the strength of your voice. What is the definition of quality voice regarding this therapy? It's the quality or texture of a voice produced or tone that differentiates it from other sounds that has the same pitch volume and duration.

PRONUNCIATION

In relation to the tone and volume of a voice, another aspect that is important or worth paying attention to and that deserves" needing immediate attention is how they speak in their native tongue or dialect of their own local language in other languages. The influence of dialects can influence the pronunciation of a particular language when it comes to the order. There are many languages around the world. And, depending on the dialect of culture is a result of birth. This may affect the intertribal relationship by the process of enculturation. It also affects pronunciation since it's a result of imitation the culture of a language.

It also affects the tongue of a person to a certain degree. A few individuals are free from being influenced by the sounds it produces in its tones. There are at least some widely spoken languages in the present that demand adequate amount of attention to a proper pronunciation in order for a better understanding of the sounds to give its true significance. This includes the English spoken languages; French, German, Spanish and Greek for a couple of examples but they are certainly in need of studying, and usually require a proper, accurate and authentic pronunciation to the language.

Ogoni language is a different one within the Nigeria country that requires immediate attention due to its exquisite, deep and captivating the melody of her dialect singing. A certain Ibo man recently declared that the Ogoni dialect has a strong and enticingly covered melody, which will be in exhilaration when one sees or hears the Ogoni the language singing. It's a powerful language and incredibly influential in the speaking her dialects with its lyrical display. So, in spite of different languages and other tongues that exist in the world the same, these three provide a simple instance of what we can discuss on the way we pronounce in our hidden plan for the voice entertainment patterns.

In terms of vocal training, we need to recognize any possible pitfalls when it comes to speaking and singing ahead. For the purpose of training in voice tongues are an essential element to be dealt to in the context of our diverse and varying cultural influences. We should sincerely be able to study the concept of "pronunciation" as it affects certain dialects of our own with regard to projection. We must address this.

PRONUNCIATION

Dictionary definitions state that it should refer to a manner in how a word in a language are said" A appropriate pronunciation will clearly define the usage of the tongue to bend, throw or bend it in order to be capable of producing in distinct the sound of a specific word the same pronunciation that is not divergent, and in order to show or convey an accurate meaning of what you actually meant to convey in public opinion and potential consumer.

Making a sound that is appropriate to any word in a suitable way or in a way that does not conflict with pronunciation is the responsibility of a sound pronunciation. The studying of a particular dialect or languages requires consulting.

Chapter 2: Phonetics

It's the practice of articulating words correctly. The English dictionary describes it as include "The study and science of speech sounds, their production and the signs used to represent them". While I'm not a phonetician, but I are interested in accurate phonetic representation.

It is a matter of the human voice's ability to produce of sounds in speech. Phonetics aids in giving an accurate sound when speaking or singing. Phonetics is also utilized to teach students about how to read properly. The program also assists those who sing, like public speaker is brought into contact with phonetic research. Additionally, it helps polish the tongue and tone of vocal voices so that they can be heard clearly and appreciated following.

INTONATION

It's the melody of speech or the pitch contour. High or low key pitch. It is the key to determine the pitch of generalization to read or talk. This is the signal for tone in the voice. A low key tone is a good indicator of the messages of love or death. It can also touch highs, valleys, and plateaus with its fluctuation in the sound. This is the use of your voice when you are the making of speech or in songs. Also, it is the quality of voice that you use when the conversation with your speech. This can be sharp, low or even soft in its tone.

Intonation can be made to sound attractive or aggressive. Find out how you can use your tonal voice in order to influence the demands of an ethical situation. Also, in other words, it is the vocal tone that produces its tone used in the production. Tones usually have a the sound that can be detected for a specific reason or reason in the course of action.

The most important thing to note is the sound one's vocals play with. Most people love to listen to broadcasters or newscasters who have excellent intonation.

It can be heard in the radio, or watching TV, with the sight action displayed.

VOICE PRODUCTION

The voice is the earliest natural ability as a tool designed by God to be used immediately. First, it is heard when laughter or crying before developing into a humans can talk since the time of birth. The same can hear from human beings who are dumb as well as those who talk. There is some tune that can be used for crying as well as singing songs within the essence of use. However, for those who are dumb who cries, when they cry, there's an inaudible vocal auditory perception of a specific or particular order.

Thus, for humans speaking the moment one is considered to have lost his or her voice implies that he/she is unable to be heard easily, even when one speaks or sings during the course of speaking.

The person in question could also sing or speak, however, not with a good sound and thus not suitable with a smooth, even tone. The voice could have been fractured or had a damage or accident to the melody when performing in harsh conditions or being overused in one manner or another. The result could be that the voice losing its original tone. In this way this voice may be deemed to be weak.

It isn't as sweet than before the battle that led to its flaw. The appealing voice tone has been dragged to a halt due to its inability to gain immediate approval from those who admire your voice. What's the issue regarding your voice? Somebody might ask. The quality of your voice is gone.

ARTICULATION

The sound of speech is articulated, which allows to a clearer and distinct "A" and not "B" sound. Additionally, it is "B" sound and not "A" sound. Articulation refers to the creation of both words and its associated sound in order for the purpose to be correctly and clearly recognized without deviation or possible divergence by your breath e.g.

Dare and Dear distinct sounds.

Fare and Fair distinctive sounds.

The sound of the voice creates the tone of singing that aids to convey the message to be conveyed. This helps speed up the comprehension and appreciation of the words for the viewers.

The process of articulation involves that individual speech sounds originate from the lips, tongue, teeth to alter the breath stream that is outgoing during the production. The word "Articulation" does not require a special term called "inflection".

INFLECTION

Inflexion or an inflection is the rising and falling of the voice during talking. It also refers to the modulation of voice changing the tone of voice to convey grammatical relationships. In order to undergo such a transformation to bend or curvature the word's form with an suffix, e.g. ed, -ing. If you alter your voice, inflection and tone takes place, it influences the rise and filling of your voice during speaking and singing, or in a simple speech production procedure. Curving or bending your tongue to indicate a connection to phrases in your speech, and particularly within the lines of your songs is an inflection that is performed in the progress.

PITCH

The term "pitch" refers to the most high or the lowest quality of tone or the sound. The more rapid the cycle of vibration more intense the sound. How do you determine pitch? Sex, age and other general movement factors may affect the pitch. In addition, the length, thickness and the degree of the vocal fold's tension and pitch are equally important to what makes the speech. This could refer to pitch in the sound of music, the singing voice, or a normal human voice with no instrumentation. The degree of pitch is the measure of highness or lowness audio quality.

So, a note that is in musical sounds could be played with its highest or lowest pitch for understanding. The instrument that is in suitable use. This can be either a human voice, or any other material item that is available. As pitch determines the volume of sound that can be produced Find a suitable pitch to both your speaking as well as singing.

PUNCTUATION

Punctuation is the art and science of placing a complete stop, commas, or other essential signs within an unwritten sentence or poem.

So, when writing in poetic or prose language the correct punctuation will help in an easier and more effective understanding of the meaning.

COMPREHENSION

The art of comprehension is the mind's ability or ability to comprehend the written or spoken word to be in a position to comprehend it. What one perceives as the message of a document in the hope of a reproduction just that simple comprehending.

The elevation of the word production with sound could help distinguish the message from the appealing power of music. An improved sound by tongues creates the necessary distinction between sounds. This helps in providing a the ability to comprehend each message within the sequence.

This lecture is the result of an individual or personal insight into the ability to sing and style of singing in order to help you understand the material more quickly.

The research findings show an that there is a similarity between voice and vocal techniques to make an acceptable public performance speaking and speech-making in the same way.

An easy understanding of this discourse is an instruction for all performers, comedians, vocalists as well as instrumentalists. The way they touch affects the sound of a certain musical note, or music key as well as the singer's sound perception.

So, after having covered a few essential areas of the voice therapy components We now need focus on the most important issue of the entire plan. Enhancing your voice's beauty as well as articulation, differentiation and pronunciation can't be achieved with out other vital aspects of voice like:

Voice grooming

Control of breath

Voice attack in songs

Voice collection in melody

The voice that is natural

The tone voice

Baritone Voice

Bass voice

Alto voice

Tenor voice

A voice that is hoarse, as well as

The voice of the nasal

It is our intention to look at these components and some of the vocal tones that sequence to see the differences and apply these tones with care when needed. Because we will be treating voice as the primary voice, we are going to be sure to reveal the weak power of voice, and provide a solutions within the order.

The failures of some people's voice can be the result that they are not empowered and groomed, or trained to build the necessary capacity or strength expected by the person performing either reading, deliver a speech, or sing in any way.

Chapter 3: Voice Grooming

Because of a certain person's unproductive and unsteady sound voice, it's essential to look after it with the help of a strong or power to the voice. The reason we call 'Voice Grooming' a an opportunity to ask. One might then question: what exactly is the term "voice grooming? It is easy to answer this question with:

Vocal grooming is the process that feeds the tone your voice in order to increase its force and strength during performances. It is also the nurturing of an inexperienced vocal sound into a pleasing mature voice sound. It is typically done through the instructor of the voice.

It could be the case of a kid or an adult that is still being taught to possess a high quality voice. It is therefore an art that uses your voice to improve its performance in the making of speech and the singing and dancing.

If someone's voice is deemed not to be in good health and it is not healthy, it can"horse" with hard or harsh sound when it is sounded. A voice that is not properly trained usually creates an unnatural sounding tone which isn't tuned to an acceptable level. An unpopular voice will never be admired or even matched with its song when it diverges.

It is therefore necessary in the reconstruction of the sound's tone. When it's been correctly created, it can be tuned to the size and level required for the purpose of. It is a process that requires certain training that must be completed to attain the highest high-quality sound that is deserved. Examples:

a. The length and expansion of the tone

b. Acceleration of the pitch of voice

C. The articulation of distinct sound creation

D. The tinniness or the fatness of the sound quality of an individual voice.

With the research above, with a righteous name there is a great deal that can be accomplished with regard to "Voice Grooming in order to improve how a voice is delivered in the singing and, more specifically, when it comes to delivering a great speech that is suitable for consumption by the public with respect to the sequence and fundamental.

BREATHE CONTROL

Controlling breath is the correct control of the voice in order to perform the right services when it comes to speaking and when singing songs performing. Commas, pauses punctuation, pauses and complete stop; all are essential elements of the process of breathing control. The way you manage your breathing can be a source of confidence for an effective speech, or even a great rendition of a exercising singing.

THE NATURE OF BREATHING

The human breathing process is quite a daily. The average human breathes approximately twenty thousand times each daily, as per study conducted.

Take an exhale. Then, you will see that your chest is expanding and lifting up slightly. Was that what you were doing? Your body is making the lungs grow. In the meantime, air flows into. Inhalation is the process of breathing, which is a different way of saying. However, when you exhale or breathe out, it will decrease your body's the volume.

Air is then pushed or sucked out. I'm not focusing on matters of inhalation or exhalation but rather breathing control, both in speech production and the singing capability that is controlled by voice during the whole process. In relation to breathing control in the context of our discussion, and when it comes to music that produces melodies and instruments to modulate sound, there are the 'Bars'. Bars define every short phrase, and sentences, which provide the control needed to understand a particular message, whether in a tune or a written phrase for it to be understood.

An effective breath control will help the breath not fluctuate and cause the performer to have an unnecessary interruption that is not needed when singing so in order to disappoint your viewers. With a complete control over the breath can be very effective when speaking and singing songs. Being able to soften the volume or increase it when is needed, makes an appropriate point regarding the control of voice too.

A few exclamatory sounds that are a need to control breath goes to these words. They often appear in music as well as in exercises for singing and in the speech processes.

Hu! Ok!

Uh Yea! Ssh

Ooh! Come on

Ooh-ooh! Hai

Wao! Ssha

Yeah! Mmh

Sei-yo! Mmhmm

Cha!

Hii, hi, ssh!

U-uh-uu:

Ho!

In this regard, breathing control can help one be aware of the exclamatory sound as an effect on and impact the message being sung or forming of the emphasis in speech. The proper breath control management gives the needed that's important to an article or speech that allows the listener to be fully aware of what they should anticipate or what could transpire during the process. The control of breath through exclamation can be helpful to clarify a report to allow for an acknowledgement.

Breathing in before speaking can provide the user a natural, easy and flexible control over the exhalation, which can help to achieve a high-quality vocal production. If one is scared or nervous about something or another then the vocal band will surely increase. If someone is similarly angry the person also has trouble controlling their breath. A lot of people have lost their voice, or lose control of breathing while they cry. It is common for people suffer from a loss of tone later on. The result quickly reveals that the lack of voice control because it effects the breathing pattern within the fundamental.

EFFICIENT BREATHING

Controlling breath to be sensitive is a matter of a few

Exercises like these:

1. Blowing your lips with a flutter, you can simulate air into them. The idea allows you to mimic racing vehicles or Lorries.

2. Recite three times.

a. A small, relaxed sound

b. A medium happy sigh

C. An enormous sigh of relief (you're anticipating to receive an "F" at a mouth class and instead you get an 'F' in the course.

It was apparent that there were two different types of breath.

1. Central deep breathing, and

2. Clavicular - breathing in the shoulder

The first one is raising and dropping of shoulders and collarbones. The second one is breathing in the abdominal region. The majority of people who have high-quality speaking voices as with many talented actors, performers, and athletes utilize this type of breathing as it improves the sensitivity, flexibility and comfort in breathing control, in accordance with the book "Fundamentals of Voice and Articulations" written by Lyle Mayer.

VOICE ATTACK IN SONGS

A song's message is supposed to be strong enough for the vocalist to speak exactly to what the song's message conveys. If the message is an emotional one, the voice needs to be able to convey that emotion. If the message is naturally and equally violent, it must be tuned via its tone or the voice. There is no message, there's no voice or voice, no message, should it be. Song without a purpose or function should be void.

Like every message, it have to speak through the use of a voice. This could be a tone of pen, or an action voice as a result of the the person who is performing. Concerning specifically the singing process in relation to producing music as well as the melodic sound it is necessary to have some experience before being able to provide a critique about a more effective vocal capability when responding to a vocal attacks in music.

A lot of people have high vocal quality, but some have weak voices too. Some of the poor voices of singers aren't due to the fact that the sound is not of high quality they produce, but due to the lack of control and articulation.

Usually, people use inappropriate language that is used in everyday life. They may use inappropriate words without regard to their conscience or their public perception. When they do this, in the music, also are at risk of destroying their credibility in front of the public.

Thus, using the voice when singing is a method of melody, or a technique to empower ones voice to sing songs which need to be sung in a specific date. It has been observed in the instrumentation of sound too. There are songs that aren't suited to a loud note of the instrumentation to kick off the music.

If the songs are performed with a more sluggish quality of sound the song loses its value, and throws off the intended message into insignificance. Songs that feature vocals require an understanding of the lyrics and also the used or necessary melody that is used for accompanying music.

Also, a specific character in a track may need a different vibrant tone to convey the message that the song is trying to convey. This is why there's an understanding of a vocal attack within songs. You can suggest a tune that is apt to accompany a specific track today. Your message will be communicated and its well-deserved tune.

Certain people are able to make their arguments convincing even when the goal is to prove that they are insane. They can be a magnet for others into their world. The information you don't want to divulge is easily retrieved through a clear voice. In the same circumstance, it's like singing a song with a vocal attack in relation to using the voice in order for the message to be communicated in a beautiful manner.

Find out how you can approach your songs in order to influence your listeners for the possibility of a shift in tone through your vocal.

VOICE COLLECTION IN MELODY

Human voices are the most stunning instrument on the planet. The sound that is able to reach the heart of humanity is an additional human voice. The sound can come from the cry of a child, singing, begging and begging, or asking for help, even whistling.

If a person is annoyed, it affects emotions, as it does to make curses, reprimands or the like. Other vulgar words are also acceptable.

Every human being can either curse or bless influence another person, which is why it's one of one of the most important elements that manage vocal tone! Speech pathologists can offer more help or provide a proof of this assertion or even a doctor in the same manner.

However, it is possible that there's certain characters that be a part of a human voice. As well as I can tell I have not personally conducted a tiny voice experiments, when you awaken people early, say around two and five in the beginning of the morning The voice of some people change depending on how they are speaking. It's not exactly similar by 7 hour time of the same day. I've observed that individuals' voice changes around midnight at 12:00 every day, before the next days ahead.

While these voices possess their own distinct style of speaking, certain people maintain the typical sound and his individual tone of production. As we're talking about vocals and their melody collection Let me show us other voices that make the use of unfavorable qualities, but do not go into the depths.

Some experts say that as fingerprints, every one of us has a distinct voice. unique voice. This includes:

1. Breathing Voice: fuzzy, quiet or exuding breath, which is disappearing clearly. It is usually too soft, and it does not sound strong.

2. Strident is Tense, hard and often generally a higher pitched the tone.

3. Harsh: rough at times and extremely low pitched.

4. Nasal: It's similar to talking with your nostrils, or a nasal clang. Country music artists have similar voice qualities.

5. Hoarse: loud or scratchy, it can be strained and even swollen. It's like the person who is in possession needs to clean the throat of the most basic sense.

A few of them appear natural, but some individuals may acquire these voices through imitation or practices. Let's continue.

There are a lot of people with a voice whose tone voice has a high quality in both volume as well as the melody that is coated and listened to. It is called a good voice on the microphone'. When people use microphones and speak into them the microphone, they have a pleasant quality of sound in its creation.

Additionally it is true that there are people who are able to distinguish their tone of voices based on their unique voice, but when paired with the microphone, they produce poor sound high-quality in the perception. This is because they suffer from poor microphone voices. The voices of these people may lack depth and tone, so without some guidance they may not benefit from better use in this process.

Thus, voice training is essential for these people to improve their skills for making a great

the use of their own natural vocal tone. The voices of these people aren't equipped with the appropriate note of melody to support their already rich natural voice. Although these types of voices can speak in a reasonable sound, they do not have the sweetness of melodic sound to draw the attention of people with any spoken word, either for speech and the singing of songs. If one's voice is found unsatisfactory then it's time to develop the voice naturally by undergoing a voice-training clinic in order to improve a positive company, particularly that of other voices singing to help create the required harmony during the performance. The use of one's voice in capturing certain melodies requires appropriate training so that you are capable of recognizing the voice that is before yours. An instructor of voice or trainer can assist in training your ears to perceive and listen of sounds in accordance with music progression in the production of tone the application.

Chapter 4: Anger And Voice

Also, in normal speech, the manner in which you speak or pronounce words differs when you are during anger. It is common for people to lose their natural tone in anger. It is due to the influence of anger on the voice naturally. A voice that oozes out coming from a soul that is angry won't carry any melodies to its sound. It is due to the fact that the voice has been elevated higher than the standard speech band in order to enhance the abuse or whatever really aggravates the annoyance.

Like when a great footballer is sacked by the opposition on the field or in the church, any preacher, artiste or teachers and comedians as well as actors or actresses can be expected to do their best but not to the same level. The comedians who perform in this category have a tendency to be chaotic. The singers are usually not able to sing their lines of music and could be unable to sing. The preachers aren't left out. They may be susceptible to a diversion. The tone of their voice usually changes. The messages they convey are typically taken out in their essence.

Teachers can be sure to stop the class very fast. You can also throw your chalk, or even a small sticks or staffs with his or her to the cause of anger. In this way, the comedian seems to possess a distinct attitude to preachers in this discussion. In order to regain his place as a performer, comedians have also employ anger in order in order to entertain. Many will twist their tongues, play with their voices and continue to make their voices sound shakier in order to create the audience smile by presenting a range of. These are all to create the point of dramatizing their talents. Be sure that your collection of voices is a good example of the qualities which can influence the public's perception of your voice in the present. In spite of your frustration it is your voice's responsibility to use is to implement an actual display in your collection. What happens to a soccer player in his response? Of course it is on the field. The majority of the time, he misses an excellent play. In addition, he misses a perfect pass several times. He may get either a red or yellow warning for poor play due to personal rage.

The person who is the master of ceremonies is also a category where they are subject to some form of resentment during their performances. They have to! The master of ceremonies alias the Mr. MC has every gut to get annoyed over an insensitive utterance of the general public, giving him instructions on what he should do or how he been unable to accomplish. The MCs receive a myriad of requests concerning what to do or what to say in essential. The artist is often confronted as if the opponent can do better than him.

All in all, a professional master of ceremonies needs to be aware that language is not always solid and stable. Changes and stories that could be a mix of between languages. The master of ceremonies (MC) are similar to comics. The ideal master of ceremonies is one who is funny as well as an imitation of.

The actor should be able to draw attention to a dull scene or an audience. Make a scene more lively and make an exaggeration an actuality. Should be a person with a plethora of jokes and riddles that will awaken sleepy minds, and soothe some sour hearts. He should also be able to celebrate his audience with continuous laughter.

VOICE IN DIVERSITIES

The voice of a human being is their normal unique tone of voice used the speech process or singing exercises, while moving speaking or talking, to shout, or even when performing a song. If one's voice is controlled, it may be heard in any of the voices previously mentioned above to provide the necessary melody that can be listened to by the one who produced that sounds or by any listener.

Certain people possess a high quality tone of voice while others are not so good high-quality ones. So there's no need alarm over vocal possession.

God chose to create it in this manner to serve a specific purpose in comparison to other performers. The voice may be sexy or a beautiful voice.

It is possible to classify this voice as a distinct grouping when performing different tasks. The voices can be distinguished that when they are in contact with other, they produce a harmonious sound as a result of music recognition. It is the sound of a single production that is not influenced by other voices in harmony. The individual sings or speaks according to its own preferences with a melody and tone and without question, even when they are not asked to add a sound the other. The individual in question does not need of harmony or sense since it is only in tonal.

The voice that is natural can be different tones in another group, however when it is required to mix with another voice, it is extremely expected to generate an acceptable tune in an acceptable tone of the hearing. If the desired result cannot be realized, it's later questioned for the harmony is not created or established. The two natural voices might need some instruction in order to reach a certain goal from the voice coach or instructor of music to achieve what they want or expect to get as a results.

In the event that this natural voice doesn't have ability because it's not groomed, polished or tuned for the public's consumption and acceptance with its voice The voice needs adequate amount of attention to ensure that it is properly groomed.

TREMBLE VOICE.

The sound of trembling is an appropriate and pleasant first voice. Very audible for human beings, particularly younger girls and boys. Treble voices are obviously beautiful, with the layered melody that it produces when it comes to speech and singing as well. It is more vibrant at a young age than it is producing music, as it has the attracts with its exquisite melodies within the perception of tone.

The unique treble-voiced combination is a magnet for attention when it is used in romantic songs or services. Youths with tremble voice older than their age can create mixed tones, as if distinct parts of the voice are added in the variety of tones that you can hear.

If a mature treble tone is sold when accompanied by a superb alto, it will be an impressive harmony sound in the best quality. Treble vocals are considered as the most powerful human voice for leading melodies for solo singer, resulting in an unbeatable level of comfort. It is the case when a regular sound has been used in the singing process.

It's neither sharp, or too small, nor too low to be perceived Therefore, it is very distinct and provides the correct articulation in conjunction with the text of the message being fully perceived.

The voice of the treble is by far the most commonly heard tone or sound for many people.

While a small number of individuals have an ear for bass, the tone of treble generally delivers every singing to the satisfactory melodic quality. The sound of treble that fluctuates indicates the age of the individual singing Two things can be discernible in an unsatisfactory rendition.

1. The performance's age as well as

2. The voice is the strength of the artist.

The sequence is either the person performing is underage or is very old in nature. It could be a young child from the age of five years and at times 14 years old. A lot of children in this stage do not perform as well because of the control of their breath. They're still not mature in the way they speak. Although, some children appear to be able to do it effectively and it's even better when they are 15 to 7 years old.

In contrast there are people who decrease the power of their voice as time passes. The diminished strength can cause the person change the way they sing because of a weakening in the voice's tone.

The person with a long-standing condition who falls into this category will not produce an impressive voice because of the decline for the control of breath.

Treble voice provides easy breath control due to the harmony of both exhalation and exhalation exercises, which takes place within the sequence. When you talk or sing with no strain in your voice the easy tone that lets an unbeatable, balanced sound and a relaxed breathing is the treble sound you use to express your voice. Treble tone can be described as a less frequency of sound than that of the soprano voice. Learn to sing using the sound of treble tone ahead of the other people.

TONES OF VOICES

BARITONE VOICE

The aritone voice is male in between a tenor and bass tone. The aritone voice is very rare in a few

cases. It is rare for anyone with this well-known and prestigious voice. Baritone singers are able to work using sopranos more effectively than many voices to create a flawless blend and harmony. Baritones can be located in the bass range that also has a distinctive Sound sound for accompanying melodies.

Many music enthusiasts appreciate the tone of this particular voice and have tried to replicate it as best they can. Baritone singers who have been educated require skill and improvement, which is why they have a good and distinctive appearance at concerts that are open to the public.

BASS VOICE

Bass voice definitely is an edgier and male sound that is evident in the tone of production. The males have been noted for their basses voices because they sound natural and dominant within this particular category of tones.

Bass is the smallest part of music. Bass is available and it is equally effective in the instrument and voice sound. There are also instruments with a bass sounding effects. There are women who compete with a very distinctive quality of voice. They are utilized in lieu of males in order to enhance parts of the harmony of the singing.

The bass sound wears down the aspect of melodies and can affect any singing talent when it is not accompanied by a bass instrument. Bass is a complement to the normal harmony of different melodies and voices, making it an excellent control.

Bass is the ground for landing to a myriad of different voices singing as well as instrumentation of sound. It is evident that bass is the basis for the clothing that melody gives to instruments as well as vocal renditions when it is together with others, as well as for harmony to be created in the process of the production of sound. Bass in voice and instruments is described as masculine or fatherly.

Chapter 5: Alto Voice

The male voice is called the alto. It's of the male voice that lies between the tenor and treble tone of voice. This portion of tone is called the contralto, which is the voice of women who sing. Contralto is the least female voice that sings. Take a look again: alto is the top adult male voice that is above the Tenor. The tone that is most effective when it is accompanied by an excellent treble singer. To create a perfect melodic production that is that it is acoustic and unified that it requires alto equipment.

While a small percentage of women lose tone with the tenor voice, the best voice for them is an high-pitched sound, which is the most low female voice tone.

TENOR VOICE

If one is looking to speak about the voice of an adult Tenor is the most prominent pitch male voice. If a man decides to sing using this voice this is the most normal adult voice with its most high pitch. The tenor voice is a perfect match for alto and even treble voices, for stunning melody production through its auditory perception.

While some women may engage in tenor saxophone, it is not more vibrant than men when it comes to the performance of a fine melodic tunes. Test tenor saxophone to see the way it blends with an alto sax that is so well that it is harmonious.

SOPRANO VOICE

Soprano is the most powerful vocal tone. It may be a male or female singer who is young that is in the question. This is certainly above the typical treble with regard to the frequency. Women are more likely to be heard in it, more so than male counterparts. Soprano can be best accompanied by the baritone voice when performance of classical pieces of music.

The duo will only be entertaining only if they've been properly taught in the essence. Can you recognize your voice in the manner of a singer who sings soprano? Soprano singing has a little higher pitch than the normal voice that trembles during performance.

HOARSE VOICE

It is the natural voice for some individuals. The voice is not smooth the way it perceives sound in the tone. It can be quite smooth, unnatural, rough or stressed in its the tone. The person who has this strained voice can sound like they need to clean their throat frequently. It is a sign that the windpipe in the mouth of the person needs to be cleared.

While one might be able to be able to hear and comprehend the words of the Sound, many hoarse voice sounds are acrid but they are not completely faded out. World-renowned singers are able to sing this style of voice that is beautiful to admiration.

If a voice is hoarse like a simple speaking, it's rather dry. However, when singing, it is possible to be amazed by the spontaneity of its voice. The majority of hoarse voices aren't easy to imitate due to the unique tone design. The voice of this kind is in the same category as other voices and is essential in the catalogue of tone that music professionals use for every generation.

VOICE AND MELODY

A lot of people have gorgeous voice when speaking or making speeches. It is fascinating to realize that each human owns a voice that is a sign of appreciation for the difference they make to other people.

This is your unique identity, calling card or telephone number. It could be a pleasant in its tone, or unpleasing with its production of sound. It is your own voice and you already know it.

Although some individuals dislike their voice's tone but many people do like their voices. There are voices that lack pleasing melody, while others sound beautiful even when they are not singing. However, do you know that not all the beautiful voices sound the same while singing? It could be due to not being taught correct usage and control. The first known tone of voice that is present in each human being is that of a cry, or a crying voice. The first time when a baby is born. Following this, is the sound of laughter?

After those two natural sounds the next issue is the sound of singing. The sound is certainly infused with emotion or happiness that's evidently understood only by the child or anyone who's so enthused. It is also the initial sound that is created by crying. It's generally accompanied by fluctuations in the pulse rhythm in melodic accompaniment.

Once it is more mature by the process of progress, the story shifts. The voice was enhanced by time and experience and a gradual improvement of its sound and tone is evident.

NATURALLY

Every human being has the capacity to smile, laugh, or cry. In spite of the normal breathing patterns of every living creature, some do make a sounds, while others make the sound of singing. Other people cannot be said to laugh or cry. However, we do believe that they sing.

When you look at this line of studies, one could simply talk about the singing bird, whispering cricket or crying Wolf. The only human being who could be said to have a connection with laughter as he is an god-image of God and is a higher-level of intellect.

In a close examination of the melody and voice as to singing and voice it is possible to distinguish in both its tone and the way it is applied. Melody is a key ingredient in enhancement of voice. Thus, a voice that sings is a significant difference from the ordinary voice.

The addition of melody to your voice requires training and maturation when it comes to tone display. The ability to tune your voice's tone can be a way to incorporate the melody. A singing voice is not a melody, just as one's voice with no melody cannot be appreciated in its the core. So, both voice and melody can't exist without one another. If the voice doesn't produce melodies, it were to be that of a foe. Since no enemy's voice will sounds sweet or pleasant for its adversaries at all. He smiles...

Chapter 6: How To Maintain

YOUR VOICE

Many individuals have succeeded in shaming their voice or the tone of their voice by the natural sound. In the same way, a few are extremely pleased with their voice, but with no improvement in their usage. A lot of people have been wondering about the problem and have suggested various diagnoses in order to find the best solution that will allow for the quality of the voice's tone.

There are many who are being given incorrect guidance on how to make a difference regarding their voice, but there is no solution or information to support it.

A lot of people have questioned me with regards to what activities to engage in, what that they can eat in order to enhance the voice of their choice. Many have even shared the advice of someone else to improve their voice and for essential maintaining for their voices.

I'm sure that my voice is in good shape judging by the many questions poured at my voice. It is my intention to say that I'm not entirely happy with the voice I have and am hoping to have another's gorgeous tone that I heard. Yet, somehow, you must be right now and give thanks acknowledge those seeking tips and suggestions by observing my own experiences.

Some have requested that I help them in the people who have a bad experience as regarding singing and voice instruction. It is my request in the moment, and it's your responsibility to follow these guidelines and be consistent the same in your application.

YOUR VOICE MAINTENANCE

You're one of a kind of thing, very individual and distinct in tone or the production of tone. So, for the sake of your own;

1. Our voices aren't exactly identical

2. Our individual breathing pattern isn't the exact

3. Each tone's voice comes with a high-quality sound.

4. There's a sort of melodic note in every voice

5. Each voice is great by itself

6. The distinctiveness of our voices is the variety of melodies creating

It is now possible to agree what I am saying about the seven factors listed below that impact our voices individually in categories the quality, tone or when it comes to perception. All of this in the forefront of your thoughts will give you the possibility to search for an environment where you can get trained to keep your voice in good shape. Maintaining your voice is to ensure that you must avoid interaction with any other unimportant things in order to maintain your voice healthy and in good form during the course of.

YOUR VOICE IN GEAR

1. When you sing or are a preacher, you should not shout over your usual speech range or over the normal tone and pitch that you use in your vocal. I.e. how high your voice sounds.

2. If you are a singer or preacher who is climbing to an extremely high pitch and your voice can distort or compress the mellow sound, causing the bridge between a crisp audio signal on Perception that can't be heard.

3. Intense stomach can hamper a proper breath control that will allow for pulse imbalances in its release.

4. Foods rich in oil can help raise the voice of a person to an octave that he or might not maintain during the same manner.

5. Fried food is a bad medicine for a voice that isn't trained they can increase the richness of tone. The result is a sound that is shaky or creates a it to a cough even when performing.

6. If you don't practice it, there's an insufficient expansion of the breathing and lungs, or breath intake inside the chest region. This is to enhance inhalation and exhalation exercises when singing or talking.

7. Try not to try and imitate other the voices of others, rather than using your own chosen one.

All in all, there are many other useful applications to expand the voice in the areas of breath control and maintenance, which aren't discussed here because of absence of time. Voice trainers can assist more than printed pages. Learn and follow the as far listed therapies to have better and productive engagements now.

SINGING WITHOUT INSTRUMENTATION

Voice was the first instrument God designed to sing praises to God, much like teeth were the first knife to be used by the hands of men. In the event that a child or adult human is tempted to sing or cry the melody is there as well as an instrument for singing. Also, there is an underlying rhythmic sound that acts that acts as a backdrop for the movements of sound on hearing.

These are all carried out without using any instrument or objects that is in the way or subject to question. This is because the human voice can be sung so beautifully without the use of instruments, rather than singing with a normal human voice. It is singing with no instrumentation as a process. When singing with no instrumentation, you need the ability to articulate and control. Voices that can be heard to discern an instrument's accompaniment but without physically seeing them.

If they do not possess an accurate musical rhythm they are not able to maintain this type of singing, without straying away from the source of orchestrated audio production. The rhythmic changes that fluctuate in the melody is easily noticed by the vocalist.

Although some individuals can sing better on their own without musical instruments However, there are numerous individuals who can't perform better with a direction instrument. They are those who require urgent instruction. Certain songs that call for silence for better comprehension and understanding of the message.

The same is true for those who require excellent and high-quality instruments for effectively convey the message. If one has had correct voice grooming treatment no matter the instrument or not one is capable of expressing to a greater extent the message that needs that is recognized.

Your vocal attack when handling your vocals is the best solution for an effective rendition on anxiety. Certain songs require the use of no instruments, and some that need it for faster absorption and spiritual enlightenment. So, learn to sing on your own without instruments and also learn to sing using any instrument of music, too.

HOW TO DO IT

1. Learning to sing solfa can be extremely helpful if you've been instructed about this and are able to sing it on your own.

2. Learn a song that you know so that you can sing just as the original owner.

3. Sing alone or to be accompanied by instruments.

DUET SINGING

It is a two-man spectacle that consists of singing. This is typically used to serve reasons of harmony musically in order to achieve a perfect tune. It is more entertaining than sing-along. Duet complements each other during the melody session collection since they enhance the high-quality tone to the music it creates.

The majority of them are expected to transmit a different sound through the tone of its performance because two distinct parts are within a group, therefore a lovely or gorgeous melody might be heard in the process.

When a duet has to be made using the same sound of vocals the result is sure to be a monotonous that is more perceptual more than a harmonious and fine sound.

This will create a better sound and harmony if the lower frequency of sound is paired with a higher pitch when combined with sound production displayed.

An even more stunning perception can be obtained when a higher high-pitched voice is demonstrating of sound alongside an alto voice. Another interesting idea could be achieved when the alto and tenor voices equally become a part of the performance.

Duet vocalists should recognize and accept the notion of singing while maintaining of their own tones of singing, while diverging from each other to produce an art form of power melody when entertaining their listeners.

Chapter 7: How To Follow Instruments
IN SINGING

A lot of people have found it challenging to sing to any musical instrument such as piano, guitar,

Drum and flute or perhaps a gong. These instruments, when employed with a controlling of the rhythm, will help to create a strong rhythm and follow-up. To achieve our primary goal of singing with a follow-up using any instrument, it is necessary to master a particular techniques for the practice of rhythmic control:

1. Rhythmic Progression:

Tap your feet on the ground, you can get an inch of control.

It is the motion of the melody through audio perception. The majority of the time, this is done by vocalizations and without the use of any instruments. The listeners can see what is the kind of sound or noise that you're creating. You can even begin singing in their own mind.

2. Maintenance of Beats:

How you keep the rhythmic beats within you determines what your audience will be able to take part in the singing. If you are able to maintain the correct timing for your vocals is in a rhythm, the signature will be well-balanced or very easy to adhere to.

3. Your Sequence in Control:

If you speak or sing without pauses in order to maintain an uncontrollable rate, the listeners can get what you're speaking. In the absence of respect for your speed when you speak or during speech, or when performing without punctuation, not a one is able to pay attention for long. It could have led to some other thing or surely insane. It's a bit different in comparison to the typical speech exercise or inspiration for singing.

Thus, observing every instrument that is singing is a different technique of musical contour. This involves calculating timing, controlling rhythm and the observance of stops, pauses, and slurs as well as full stops when and as needed. This can only be accomplished through the practice of a musician instructor who will guide you through a series of steps to maturation to perfection in your performance. It is therefore possible for you to learn each of the techniques or methods that have been mentioned in the past through a practiced application of the note, not just on paper pages as a theoretical basis.

An effective voice trainer can offer a great deal of assistance to beginners for how to attain the desired goal once put in motion. An idea is not intended for a contest to become an obligation.

DECLARE THE WAR AND FINISH THE BATTLE

Make sure you are putting your all into your vocals or speech-making. Take on any circumstance either to communicate or sing. Every time, you encounter a situation, inquire to God to direct the situation and the requirements in that particular time. Avoid imitating people using your voice, but just be you If you don't, you'll eventually fall. Be aware of your natural voice and make use of it.

Are you planning to lead by singing or through a public speaking event? Learn the correct pitch at the beginning. Your style and presentation should be in the same way as you normally do. It's difficult to appear naturally natural to your audience. Get rid of that mountain of shame, fear and insecurity. Be confident and know that you're the sole person in that space. The actors and actresses are aware of this, particularly when they are required to perform an on stage performance. They are not exempt as their peers within the context. The same goes for preachers.

Of course you've declared conflict, and you have to finish the war. What's the war? Your message is at the ready. Language is a platform for the reader to cross while your choices of words are the bullets. Kill it using it. You can also uproot it. It could be a source of praise or a harsh rebuke of a bad execution on the application.

HOW TO GAIN YOUR AUDIENCE

WHILE SPEAKING

First step in order to build your audiences who are ready to hear and see your message is to:

1. You should be ready and enthusiastic to entertain, stir and make them feel welcome by presenting with a sense of humor whether in action or speech.

2. Check out the scene to record the scene on the ground to rapidly complement the already Perforated Scene or Arena.

3. It's not about what you are aware of that is important it's what you wish your audience to

understand or document that's important or is necessary.

4. If you're in the audience prior to your presentation then it is quite simple for you to figure out what to do next. to date with the audience.

5. Did you hear a lot of noise or even a lot of silence prior to your appearance on stage? Understanding the goal you want to begin with will help you establish the ability to listen well to your character.

By incorporating these suggestions or information for your presentation can ensure you have a huge performance that will really impress your public's attention while performing.

Your ability to talk is not important, but the anointing and the baptism of God's Spirit on your words. Make sure you break yourself of self-consciousness But remember that you are God who is in that time. If you've prepared your speeches or songs correctly, it is certain that the rain will pour down; the sun will shine, and the wind will flow, all of which will enhance your skills or talents in the display. When you're a performer, rehearsal of your songs will help the lines to pop with your impressive singing. Your audience should be assured that they will get the item they desire. However, do you really know that they are the ones for whom and you're in the right place? If not, then be humorous when it is required and be sober when it calls for and also have fun when you are delivering your communication.

You may be entertainer, and you are also an ambassador, then let it all be.

WHO MATTERS?

The person who knows you doesn't have any significance. The person who invited you to the party is not important, but the one who invited to you for ministry is important. Let Him know what you would like God to accomplish for you, and let Him decide the things He might not want to accomplish.

God is a man of many talents and is able to do whatever is unable to accomplish something, for his glory, honor and praise. God is an excellent calculator and timer that is not normal.

HOW TO GAIN YOUR AUDIENCE PROPER

1. It is only possible to gain target audience when they discover something that they've not previously heard.

2. It is also possible to win your viewers when they start to look at what they've previously not experienced.

3. The audience will appreciate your message greater when they achieve what they were unable to have done before.

4. Your audience will appreciate you even more if they obtain something that they've previously not received previously. Moreover:

5. Listeners will be able to sustain you by being successful in removing sorrow and instill joy in the event that you've been

capable of removing hatred in order to create love, and you've managed to help the hurting.

Chapter 8: A Good Voice Entertains

A great voice makes a great sound. An unresonant sound does not have a good tune or tone of it's by itself. If a voice has had some attention and care by being groomed and conditioned, it is sure to be pleasing in its tone and voice in its high-quality.

Voice therapists can help an extremely weak voice to develop volumes and strength that could become a source of entertainment. It is possible to say that they were satisfied today if the voice of a professional comes in conversation with a compelling narrative. Many users have felt dissatisfied when an excellent story is delivered by a weak storytelling voice with a tone. With a clear pronunciation and an excellent habit of using phonetics effectively, many are thrown into joy when their voice communicates. A person's natural tone of voice may entice them to the point that they may be unable to control the urge in order to applaud the presenter. Sometimes, this happens without any system in place that can ensure a clear sounding instruments.

A great microphone's voice is more enjoyable than the normal voice tone at the core. Be gentle and don't shout when trying to deliver an ordinary speech. Keep your voice soft for a better sound on the microphones.

COMMUNICATION SPELL

In order to tackle this subject properly for a proper understanding, you must have an understanding of the meanings of the two terms "Communication and Spell" on the subject to ensure the importance of voice capability in speech.

In that case, what does communication mean? It's simply the act of communicating or passing the information or facts from one side one end to another. It can also mean to express emotions, illnesses, heat movement or any other kind of passing on to someone or to something which could influence transmitting.

The same way the word "spell" is employed as a charm, or a belief that it has magical abilities that go beyond the imagination of anyone. An individual who has the audience in suspense has an enormous influence on the audience at the core. A spell can be described as an interest or attraction to an act of the performer or demonstration during the course of an occasion.

In the past, these two terms can be used regarding the subject that is being discussed. Communication spell is surely an appealing strength or force with the selection of words in a speech or lecture, or delivering any type of message to a crowd. It can be a an event of a religious, political or training seminar with a purpose of education. Speaking with a high level of eloquence that the speaker is able to convey using a few words can certainly enchant those in attendance or watching through one of the most effective communications exercises.

If you start to talk about real-world facts, divulge some secrets that are not known, or when you have made the dream come true for those around you, a communications spell can be cast at the audience, and they are then able to give applause to complement your presentations. Spells of communication are also created when you use your strategy to create using effective visuals and a the power of language and control. An effective language communications can be awe-inspiring to the attention of any person when the speaker has the words or words that are relevant to the message. Communication spells are also a result of from a sour heart and a sense of bewilderment trusting the speech of the speaker.

It helps to eliminate the possibility of drowsiness or sleep in the process of entertaining. This spell of communication keeps your target audience in constant contact, with no mind wandering,

The people in the LI are seated but not in the same room as the lecturer. The same thing makes it difficult for your audience be able to walk across any bridge and follow the preacher or lecturer until he has been.

Communication spell refers to a type of hypnotism, or baptism into the hyperbole terms used in express an outline of speech. Also, it acts as an anointing to transmit of a message. By doing this, the audience can be made to a receptacle through an impressive communication style and appropriate choice of words, with no qualms about what to say at the moment in moment.

A spell of communication will always keep users waiting around to hear more, so go to the next one and they'll demand. Information that is well communicated can always be liberated from distortion. In the event that communication has produced excellent information, no reservations can be made about any potential alteration. This is why information has no negative key to deform until manifest. It is now possible to say that more information leads to the transformation.

Communication spells only come from good information, there is no way for a bad situation to result in misfortune.

MICROPHONE AND THE VOICE

To discuss the above subject it is essential to be aware of the different kinds of microphones. One particular type or model will require understanding the capacity, capabilities as well as its frequencies. Because they are different in appearance and design as well, they also have different types of the sound produced.

The particular kind of device may be used but not achieving the desired outcome because of a cause. This could result from its use and manipulation by an inexperienced person who is attempting manipulating.

However, I cannot discuss all kinds of microphones but simply mention few microphones to begin my discussion on really revealing how you can use them.

Before we get started, however I'll briefly give a few examples of microphones.

1. Dynamic Microphones

2. Bi-directional Microphones

3. Wireless or cordless Microphones

4. Omni-directional Microphones and

5. Pin-up Microphones.

They are just microphones to get acknowledgment as well as enlightenment to an improved use of them and a possible control of its capabilities with regard to frequency and speed.

I'm not discussing or selling microphones in this article as a manufacturer, designer, nor a retailer, rather as an ordinary user who has for a long time worked with and dealt with many kinds in order to communicate effectively with microphones.

Sometimes as a Disc Joker (DJ) and as a Master of Ceremonies (alias) the Mr. Mc, as a singer, preacher and seminar Speaker on various occasions by using microphones. The impact of these microphones is not to be underestimated in comparison to a normal human voice when it is on displays.

Chapter 9: Know A Little Bit About Microphones

1. Dynamic Microphones

It's extremely broad in terms of frequencies. Ideal for recording music particularly in studios.

2. Bi-direction Microphones

It is a dual-directional operating kind of. It selects sound waves in two directions, with the appearance of a net. It also works equal for two people simultaneously.

3. Cordless Microphones

They are not connected to any cables. The device can make sound magnetic by its speed of the frequency. It is among the latest inventions to detect sounds at a greater space than cables and is extremely sensitive.

4. Omni-directional Microphones

The type that is described above can receive or accept sound at identical frequency in every direction. This is an older model that is frequently used for discussions on programs in studios, or for the basis of a chorus.

5. Pin-up Microphones

This microphone is powerful, and typically is hung onto the garments of any presenter or person. This is among the latest microphones designed used for entertainment or public speaking services. The microphone was designed with the basis of selfish motives for only use; it is designed for private benefit, mostly.

HOW TO USE MICROPHONES

Through all the discussions we have had so far on microphones, we might ask what exactly is a microphone? It's a device that converts electrical energy, like in radios, telephones, etc. The dictionary could be saying. However, when using a microphone is a way to boost the volume of sound when placed within a loud speaker in order for the purpose of amplifying its sound hearing. So, microphones possess some sort of velocity frequencies for the reception of sound. They are also extremely sensitive, and should you place it near your mouth, they it will block the collected wave of audio, which in turn create a travel sound which is unpleasant to ears. Certain microphones are designed for higher performance and greater strength consequently, these require greater manipulation and control in order to ensure a long-lasting effect. Many users who are new to using microphones are not a fan of the device. Many people put it into their mouths and try in order to cut it. A few people would take over the whole surface using their mouths and even their noses when they try to

Sing or talk with it. A lot of people avoid using microphones in order to give speeches. Many will refrain from breathing into their mouths as if they pose a danger to themselves. Others will approach the issue with fear and the other hand, try to talk about the issue. Did you know that a few individuals can use it with no understanding of the significance or its purpose?

This doesn't allow the microphones to create an distinctive sound which is why they are not able to produce its sound. Many people shout when trying to speak using the microphones thinking through their shouting, people will be able to hear them more clearly. It's not the best technique or method of utilizing it.

Then, move the microphone away from your mouth for about 6 inches. Examine the volume or quality of the sound. Then, bring closer to the mouth so that you can hear and feel the sound audio signal upon the reception.

In the course of speaking or singing when you sing or talk, if your voice appears weak, try to bring it closer so that you hear the proper sound the essence. If you're able to clearly hear yourself, other people can also hear and receive your voice with clarity. Find out how you can utilize the microphones right now to ensure your future performance to be better. They're there to increase your vocal volume and more clear when it is properly utilized.

The microphone improves audio quality and reception than human voice. Additionally, it helps avoid straining your voice through its usage. Make your voice more powerful by using a microphones.

COMEDIANS AND THE AUDIENCE

Before tackling the subject mentioned above, it is important to be aware of who comedians are before deciding on what he does.

can affect his viewers and the wider society by influencing certain related affects his audience and society through certain related. The meaning of the dictionary is as "actor who performs comic roles in broadcasts or plays:

someone who acts with humor and is not thought of as serious'.

What is the current state of comedy? The definition of comedy in the dictionary is, "Branch of drama that deals with everyday life and humorous events" On the basis of this, one could explain that comedy isn't a tragedy and it isn't a welcomed thing in any way. What comedy is as is a positive development of amusement and humor comedy, jokes, and entertainment in all Sorts.

Thus, a discussion of comics and their audience is sure to call for associated events which could result to joy, happiness laughter, fun, and also entertainment. It is possible to remove some of the immediate grief and sorrow to result into laughter and peace of body, spirit and soul throughout the course.

For entertainers, amusers or comedians the things people would have expected, to be the essence of laughter include smiles, joy and screams of amazement. an eerie hypnotism resulting from a flawless display and most importantly, the ability to communicate.

Comedy or comedians is merely a collection of abilities that God is putting together for enjoyment and joyous celebration as a gift that is unique to the individual or people to maintain the peace of mind that is required within the context of a world. "Every good gift and every perfect gift is from above, and cometh down from the father of lights, with whom is no variableness, neither shadow of turning" (James 1:17).

The same can be said for the audience that comedians too are an opportunity for our society in order to make us feel sad or angry about human situations. However, what is the current state in the comedians of today, especially in the United States currently? They've strayed from the norm into some sexually explicit, vulgar and blatant abuse of sacredness, and have been preaching sexuality to justify our social unhealthy consumption. These comedians who are a part of our time have taken it into the extreme of aiding in the slumber of our homes, families kids, neighbors and friends in the name of entertainment, and they have claimed to do so. Many vulgar languages are currently being incorporated into the system, without regret, shame, or even apology.

The sloppy narration of stories used that support an idea make it even more violent and threatening for the devil to get more keen on morals of society. What kind of unwelcome display will scare an intelligent brain? What is a show that can be successful in promoting shame and humiliation? It's a pathetic and hopeless thing that could quickly split families? What is a sexist utterance that causes disorganization, displacement and sabotage the foundation of our holy and righteous minds, environments and spaces? What will the kids gain by this kind of present that is based on a sane purpose display?

This is a way of asking all moral Christians as well as morally-minded individuals as well as law-abiding citizens in addition, our competent government to investigate or restrict and conduct a sound review of this type of high-corruption and immoral music similar to the majority of music which also displays utter brutality on the Nigeria Television screens to avoid an immediate ruin of our country. The comedians who are dragged into this particular aspect of their productions and performances are therefore warned and urged to stay clear of this, otherwise a judgement balance hangs in the balance. Do you think it is for financial gain or is it because with out vulgar, offensive and sexy languages, no one could afford to purchase your DVDs or video Cassettes? Turn around and accept God as the source of your gifts and talents, and you'll be greatly blessed.

In the end, it's just difficult to make others smile or be awed by your talents. It's not due to your strength or skill, however God who loves every star is able to make you shine. (Deut. 8:18). In all the discussions we have had so far I'm not in any way commissioned to demonize, attack or slander you and hinder the market for you as a singer or Comedian. I am only to offer suggestions on how to build prepare your career with faith in God praise, public praise and praise.

COMEDIANS AND THE CHURCH

There is great concern to hear of comics who go to great lengths to make fun of the Church in the name of Jesus Christ like in terms of corporate organizations. Also, it is the bleak side of having the God's name God in a way that is blasted without consideration of His judgemental morality and holiness that must not be questioned with even little or no humour.

What is the reason that someone, in the interest of having fun risk his own life just for the sake of having the most of his time or make some entertainment through making someone smile. Don't make a joke about things related to God or his ministers of the Gospel in order to make people feel better about themselves and be able to appreciate an unprofessional behavior by you.

Every comedian is hereby cautioned and then advised to stay clear of the entertainment of the church's arenas as well as its message and particularly God and his Servants so as to avoid incurring any hurt in their lives.

Weddings and ceremonies are not required. need the kind of entertainment that is a denial of the authority of a holy, righteous God.

Chapter 10: The Broardcaster

Talking about a broadcaster means an act of broadcasting. which is a method of dissemination in order to announce, declare, announce or announce news or information about things or about something. The narration of information that calls for information, using the means of engage, educate and educate our society. Thus, a broadcaster certainly an announcer. He talks, reads or broadcasts stories as information for the general public.

He or she must have been an educated person or actor who is now an organization, body such as a radio station, or TV station. The person should have received professional's knowledge of how to handle speech announcements, news bulletins or written comments for effective way to communicate the news as well as any other issues that are in the spotlight for public relations.

The broadcaster could therefore be considered to be the gossip or teller, or newscaster simply because they carry information from one quarter to the next for revenue. The person who broadcasts is a skilled talker who is aware of the elements of his words to be used during a certain date and time. An experienced broadcaster is more knowledgeable and knows about the specific seasons and timings in regards to the type of songs and phrases to be used during each hour of the day during the time of each show, even while working. It is usually the case for announcers and is not applicable to other employees of the institution.

In the Christmas season, they ensure that there is no other Christmas music not appropriate for the time of year is ever played, so it is a false reference for such a time in the time. Also, in the same manner would an Easter-themed song can be broadcast in the festive season.

Watching this conduct be maintained is proof that educated, skilled broadcaster is on the right track.

There are a few rules of any skilled and well-trained broadcaster while broadcasting, both music and news, regardless of the circumstance or power behind the broadcast. These include personal insults as well as image denting and an libel claim. All music that also promotes nakedness and exposes divinity of human beings according to a degrading spiritual norm should be absconded from otherwise someone accused of one's persona can be sued for it.

Even with all of the discussion that has been made so far by the media, what do we see and hearing about on the local and national radio and TV stations? The nakedness of girls, females and even ladies is contaminating and contaminating our view. It is believed that gentlemen are in sexual promiscuity, with a high level of propensity. If only moral persons question the quality of trading in our two states as well as national service providers for the sake of style and entertainment through our screens on television and radio What will God the Almighty Jehovah God declare regarding the moral standards which has been violated during the course of the course of it?

WE CAN REPENT AND CHANGE

It is time to wake us from our slumbers of spirituality to revive the positive morals that we had in the past to our current society. Beware of the usage of porous substances that could encourage further insanity to the system of our nation.

Let both Radio as well as our Television stations drop those discs and music videos which are a source of corruption for our homes, children's communities and families. When it comes to broadcasting, I think there are still some things that is known as N.T.B.B. A N.T.B.B is an item that should never be broadcast as well as heard or seen, nor should it utilized to broadcast. The Professional

Ethics series that is a requirement in broadcasting of any item which should not be broadcast during a broadcast.

What exactly is N.T.B.B? It's just "Not To be Broadcast' The abbreviation is regarded as potentially dangerous content for broadcasting that could be threatening or threatening to human consumption. The kind of material that is banned can be anything from personal insults which can harm someone's reputation as well as any other music which promotes nakedness while doing so.

However, in broadcasting there are many other departments, like News Department, Engineering Department, Music Department, Talks drama, religious and Commercials as well. They are all part of broadcasting as a whole. All through, the broadcasting is a show that plays out most of the flavor or tunes to the social scene. They're the ones responsible for every blemish or praise that any broadcaster would transmit in the Radio or TV houses across the globe. Presenters at these prestigious institutions come from the department of programmes or division within these communication institutions. Thus, the life of society of the society is based on the broadcasting of any programs are aired on these broadcasting companies. That means the overall management of these stations is always in the loop for every crime that is aired in any television channel today. What are they able to do, other more than restrict the presenters' individual appearances to be guided and warned before they go during the broadcast and play only the content that will aid in reducing the stigma with regard to these moral depravities.

"Who is aware of the judgement of God and the fact that they who engage in such actions are worthy of dying, they not only perform the same yet take pleasure in doing them", Rom.

1:32.

This morning, our morals was shattered, so make an end to this in your broadcast. Please don't broadcast naked human-made films or videos in public broadcasts and God will be greatly honored and exalted.

The people who create these game of shambling own their own private television stations. If they don't cease, they will have to face the consequences of the matter. And our screen that we are viewing. If you are adamant and do refuse to give up, then you're one of them. It is true that radio stations are meant to teach, inform, and entertain, yes sure, but is everything we are hearing and seeing about this? Change the direction of our country to benefit. Let's bring in more lively enlightenment programs that we can watch on our television and radio screens. Our children will become a well-rounded, intelligent and a thriving society to be a decent and god-fearing future in the case of unborn children.

Chapter 11: Music Theory

How can we talk about the theory of music in a book about voice instruction? This is due to the fact the fact that I wrote this book as a comprehensive package for aspiring singers to be a professional and cutting this chapter out does not meet that objective.

It is important to note that if you're familiar with these fundamental principles, then skip this chapter and move right into chapter three.

Let's now define a few Musical terms that every musician must know and that includes singers too:

Notes

Music is composed of sound. The word "note" refers to any sound made in music. The alphabet is used to identify these sound. The Alphabet in the field of music is not all of the letters in the English Alphabet, but we will use a subset of only seven (7) alphabets of The English Alphabet.

For example as ABCDEFG

Observations:

It is evident that

Piano begins with the note C.

The keys in black are placed with patterns that include two's and three's.

The keyboard of this piano has six C's (count by yourself).

When you locate C, it's easy to determine what the name of white notes because they are arranged alphabetically.

The note closest to the middle on the keyboard can be referred to as middle C. Find out how to distinguish this note easily.

In reality, there are only seven musical notes, white ones are the only one. the note after G A, the next note follows. A.

Scales

Scale is a Scale is an arrangement of notes that are played one after one after.

A complete step(tone) includes an accompanying note (e.g. C and D both have notes between). Half step(semitone)has zero note between (e.g. E and F do not have a note between. Additionally, B and C also are not marked between).

Major scales are based on the following pattern: Tone Tone Semitone Tone Tone Tone Semitone

TT S T TT S

The most common way to record our Major Scale as C D E F G A B C

It is usually referred to as"Do Re Mi Fa So La Ti Do

or d r m f s l t d

Everyone who sings should know this.

Octave

A octave consists of 8 (8) major notes that form an entire musical scale. The major notes are white keys, without black keys of the keyboard. C1 to C2 could be an illustration of an Octave.

Each note of the octave have been labeled exactly the same (e.g., "C") however the frequency (pitch and high or low) in the sounds are likely to differ; the second note is a little thinner than the initial note. This is similar to the sound of a woman and a man sing at the same time. Although they're performing the same tune the one is more slender than the one.

Interval

An interval describes the relationship (or distance) between two distinct notes.

Certain notes (notes) when played, or combined simultaneously, make a delightful (sweet) mix when heard. They are believed to be harmonies. They are referred to as chords by musicians. They form the basis of musical intervals, and these "agreeable" intervals are the foundation for harmony singing, which is when the notes in a chord are played and singing together.

Any two sounds whose frequency (heard in the form of "pitch") make a 2:1 ratio can be considered to differ by an Octave. This means that two sound waves are good when played simultaneously if the first sounds has twice the frequency of the second. Similar to two sounds having five times the frequency is considered to have an interval of third. They also sound nice when played.The sound waves are pronounced

These are the natural notes (Major Notes or White Keys).

Sharp notes (#) occurs when we lift an instrument. This is a black key just to the left of a white key.

Flat notes (b) is when we lower the note. A black key that is that is directly left of a white note is a flat note.

Note (b):

MUSICAL TERMS

* Melody

A melody in music (also called voice, tune or line) is a line or a succession of notes that is not sung to be sung together as in harmony. This usually is the primary element of the song that composes.

* Harmony

This refers to the usage of notes that are different in the song. This is especially true it is when different sections are singing simultaneously by various sections of a group (soprano alto and bass, tenor and so on). Harmony differs from the melodie of the song.

Pitch

It is a reference to the perception of a music note. Humans' ability to sense pitch is correlated with the frequency sound waves picked by the ears. The sound waves are transmitted as the form of tension and compression cycles through the motion of particles within air. The more rapid stimulation of the sound will increase the frequency of sound, and results in many more cycles within a certain duration. It is a noticeable rise in the pitch. The note's pitch is measured by its frequency that is determined as hertz (Hz) (or cycles) per second.

The term pitch is used by singers and musicians. term "pitch" to refer to the sound's frequency wave. The smaller the wavelength, and the faster the vibrating, the higher frequency and the pitch. Short waves sound high, and longer waves sound lower.

Instead of being aware of all this physical laws, musicians simply name their notes on the notes they employ the most frequently. For instance, they might refer to a note as " C", for instance. (see the section on notes).

When we talk about "hearing pitch" or "singing on pitch" (or "singing on pitch"), they're referring to the ability of a person to think about and sing the notes they are supposed to hear and sing.

"Singing "on pitch" is the identical to the song "in tune" or "on key".

SIGHT-READING

Music is composed on a staff (plural staves) which is comprised of five (5) horizontal lines. The five lines make four spaces.

Spaces and lines are numbered starting from the bottom and ending at the top.

We are left with five(5) Lines, and Spaces of four (4) Spaces

The staff is separated into segments using bars. The bar lines is known as the measure

Notes are usually placed along these lines as well as spaces. These notes may be placed over them

Pitch refers to the intensity or the lowness or note

This is an illustration for Written Music or Staff notation. Do not memorize any information at this point, but just watch..

The actual structure is comprised of two staves.

one that holds one to hold the notes that are from Middle C upward, and

Another way to store one more place to store the notes starting from Middle C downward.

Other lines are also possible to be added as ledger lines.

The staff on the top is called"the TREBLE CLEF staff. The lower one is called the BASSCLEF staff. the lowest one is referred to as"the BASSCLEF Staff.

The majority of songs employ the treble clef. It is the symbol used for Treble Clef

It is also the symbol used of the Bass clarf:

This is the note for the Treble Clef (called G-clef since the curly part of the symbol is centered about G).

The Treble Clef Line's names"Every Good Boy Do Well

The space clef treble Spaces: A C E

The notes below are on the Bass Clef (called F-clef since one of the notes between 2 dots is F).

The notes below are for the bass clef lines The Giant Big Dogs Fight Always

The notes below are for the bass clef The notes on the bass clef Spaces are: The entire Cows Eat Grass

Rest

The silence in music is just as crucial as the sound. The term "rest" is used to describe it. Names and lengths for rest are identical to the notes.

The rest of the scene appears to be an opening that is in the ground.

The half rest appears to be an hat.

Timing

Everyone who sings must be aware of their how to time their music and not sing offbeat. This is known as a Time signature.

The highest number in the fraction tells you the amount of count you'll get in any given measure. The lower number tells you what type of note you will get each count. Therefore, we will count:

A good example is:

Note how the notes are arranged above the employees. If you're not sure what they mean then go to prior page and read the notes again. ....

Now let's practice what we have learnt.................turn to the next page

Take care of all the other details...

Chapter 12: Anatomy Of The Voice

The technique of singing is well-defined that is dependent on the application of

The the lungs the lungs, acting as an air supply or bellows

The larynx is a vibrator; it acts like a vibrator

The head and the head cavities. These serve been designed to function as amplifiers and tube for the head and chest cavities of a winds instrument is a tube in a wind instrument.

The tongue, along with teeth, the palate and the lips, articulates and imprint vowels and consonants in the amplified sound.

What is the process of producing sound?

The production of voice depends on the movement of air through these vocal cords (lebeofun) and then out over the lips. The sound of your voice is caused by the vibrating of the vocal cords. The two folds of your vocal cords are located in the middle of your

Adam's Apple (gogongo) and are on the horizontal side of the air tube.

The folds are open even during normal breathing. That's what happens when you attempt to sing:

The lungs pump air into the trachea, which carries it to the vocal cords

The vocal cords vibrate and make sound.

The sound is absorbed into the area between the mouth (oral) and the nose (nasal) in addition to

Jaw, teeth lips and tongue shape the sound into vowels as well as consonants. They transform it into an important melody.

Vocal Cords

The voice box vibrates and is located inside the vocal box (larynx).

The tone of a sound can be defined by the level of tension that is placed on vocal folds.

These tiny "folds" are only about what size your thumbnails are.

Some are longer or thicker over others.

After they are closed, the flow of air is stopped temporarily.

If air is flowing upwards it is separated.

The sound is created when the two meet.

If the singer sings note A4 (i.e. A above the middle C) then the cords are vibrating in 440 cycles every second (440 khz).

If a singer who isn't trained tries to make high notes sound more powerful and vocal cords are separated excessively, resulting in a

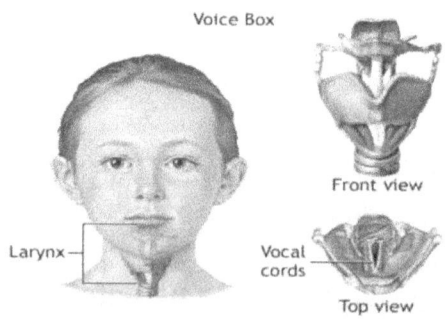

Voice Box

Larynx —

Front view

Vocal
cords

Top view

blasting" sound.

The Larynx (Voice Box)

The larynx (or the voice box) is found within the neck. It is the organ responsible for the production of sound. The airway is also protected when swallowing food, ensuring it is safe for food to not go into the lung. To find your larynx:

Make sure you touch the adam's apple (very tiny in females) and

Swallow.

Do you think of singing while you go about it? The amazing movement is guaranteed that no air, or any air or even air will pass into your vocal cords, or the lungs when swallowing anything. Our airways are extremely sensitive and in the event of a catastrophe then we'd all be dead.

Training The Larynx

Larynx is also referred to in the popular sense as the "voice box", houses the vocal cords. Making sure your larynx is neutral while singing is among the essential aspects of the field of Voice Training. The most comfortable position for the larynx can be described as the neutral location. For locating your larynx just follow these simple steps:

Breathe for a few seconds and let it as it rises. Check how high up your throat? If your larynx is raised and it constricts your vocal cords, cutting off lots of resonance room for your sound. You end up getting the term "tension.

This is the primary source of tension for people when they are trying singing higher notes. The larynx is raised because it gives false "feeling" that it will help them sing the notes at a higher pitch. Then you realize that it uncomfortable to sing notes. It is also a time to consider what the reason is for feeling like there's a lump in your throat. You know what? There's a lump in the throat of your larynx!

To neutralize the pressure on the larynx, it is necessary to practice your larynx. Personally, what I need to do is put my fingers on top of Adam's apple, when it's in a resting posture. And, when I get ready singing, I will ensure that my larynx doesn't overhang my fingers. This may be difficult initially. Don't be worried because with the right time and practice and practice, you'll have your larynx at a neutral level each time!

Activities that will help to to keep your larynx neutral:

mum-mum-mum,

buh-buh-buh, and

guh-guh-guh.

Keep an 'edgy' tone under your voice as you work the scales. When you sing these phrases, it automatically reduces the larynx. Always apply your fingers to the to the top of your Adam's Apple while doing these exercises, too.

It can take some the time necessary to train your vocal cords to remain neutral while singing. If you are able to pay attention and commit to deliberately train to improve your singing, you could accelerate the process significantly.

Once you've trained your larynx into a neutral position and neutral, you'll notice an improvement in your voice that you've never previously felt. There is less tension. Greater strength. Aren't you sure that's what every artist would like?

Chapter 13: Breath Control

Within singing there are four stages of breathing: breathing-in period (inhalation),suspension, exhalation period (phonation) and recovery period.

A healthy breathing pattern is at the heart of singing, and a good posture is the only method to properly breathe. Avoid lifting your shoulders while singing.

Similar to how you can increase the high notes you sing, as well as your vocal range, it is also possible to effortlessly control your breathing. The American Academy of Otolaryngology (Head and Neck Surgery) divides the production system into three primary elements:

Your lungs, that provide the energy source

Your voice box is the vibrator

Your nose, throat the sinuses and mouth comprising the resonance

The diaphragm, or diaphragm, is the part which inflates and deflates airways to facilitate breathing in the way we do.

As the diaphragm is lowered, it expands the ribcage and draws air into the nostrils and mouth so that it can fill up the entire lung capacity.

The moment it is raised in elevation, it compresses the rib cage and the lungs are compressed, creating an air stream through the trachea.

It's this airstream or exhalation that stimulates your vocal folds, allowing them to create your voice.

Reasons For Dysfunctional Breathing

1. Smoking causes chronic bronchitis, which is the swelling of airways that cut off the volume of air that is that is pumped out and into the lung. Smoking causes emphysema as well, lung conditions that cause the lungs to become less elastic, which makes breathing difficult via diaphragm.

2. It appears that you're breathing in the correct way and the most dysfunctional breathing habits discovered from watching the poor breathing habits of the elderly,

3. It is a common practice to spend too long sitting in a seated position, where diaphragmatic breathing gets uncomfortable. In time your body begins to lose the natural tendency to breath from the diaphragm/belly,

4. In certain instances, the diaphragm loses force, probably due to an absence of exercise/use or health issues.

For correcting your breathing pattern, understand the vital role that diaphragms play in breathing.

Understanding how this vital organ of the body functions can assist you in regulating your breathing and, consequently also your voice.

Breathing Exercises

Exercise 1: Releasing Tense Diaphragm Muscles

Exercise 2: Hearing Sound to help control your breathing. Hearing like a snake

Exercise 3: Bouncy Hissing Sounds For a More Flexible Diaphragm

Exercise 4:Panting Like a Dog

Exercise 5: Practicing Slow Breaths For Deeper Breaths

Exercise 6: Training Your Body For The Correct Singing Posture and Vocal Endurance

Breathing is not a good thing without proper posture. This is why the following Chapter...

Chapter 14: Posture

Posture can affect breathing which makes singing hard as well as bad

An upright posture helps avoid the waste of energy.

It helps create a higher level of self-confidence, confidence and self-assurance when doing.

People respond more to singing who have proper posture.

The benefits of good posture are reflected in the overall health of your body, allowing for more blood circulation, and also reducing exhaustion on the body.

As they sing, the singer should be attentive to the posture of their feet and knees, hips, the chest, abdomen as well as their hands, arms and heads. The correct positioning of these will make it much easier for the sound to be created.

There are TEN parts of the perfect standing posture for singing

The feet should be a little separated, and one should be slightly ahead of the opposite.

Knees should be loose and flexible and not locked.

Hips straight ahead, with the hips pointing upwards.

The spine is aligned

The body's weight is slightly to the left.

Straight forward with the head facing straight ahead

The chin should lie equal to the floor.

Shoulders must be secured to the side and up, while keeping your shoulders held up and not strained.

Abdomens should be flat and strong, being held in an a position that is expandable.

Hands must be relaxed, and positioned at the side.

Chapter 15: Voice Foods

If you are a singer the voice is your instrument. Just like athletes, professional vocalists maintain their vocal health and strong through vocal exercises, including breathing and warm-ups that are designed to maximize the use of their lung capacity. Certain foods may also help the voice improve.

Good Foods to Help the Voice

These are the foods good for our health and vocals. They allow us to create healthy and strong voice, as well as safeguard our vocals from damaging bacteria or viruses.

Honey will help you feel more comfortable inside your throat. It can affect your voice and make it difficult to keep the notes in check if you consume the honey too heavily. If you are suffering from a painful throat or notice something a little off in your voice, take a teaspoon of pure Honey then let it run through our throats. This can help stop the growth of bacteria as well as help the sore throats heal quicker! Apple can also help.

2. A Light Meal of Whole Grains, Protein, Fruit and Vegetables

It is essential to eat a balanced diet to ensure that you have enough power and endurance required to be confident when performing. Consume a snack every 2 or 3 hours prior to the show. Eggs, chicken, fish and rice are good for consumption prior to performing. Also, vegetables and fruits are great choices. But the citrus fruits must be avoided because they may cause dryness in the lining around the throat.

Vitamin C: Take Vitamin C tablets however, not to much. It helps to eliminate voice problems through the coating of mucus.

Drinking water is vital to drink plenty of pure water so that we can keep our bodies hydrated, and to rid our bodies of contaminants that could be accumulating within our cells and tissues. Also, it helps to keep illness and infections in check, and will help to keep a good level of overall well-being. Drink water to nourish your soul. It is not only beneficial for your voice, it is also great for overall health too. Along with hydrating the body, it also helps keep our vocal cords dry and that is crucial for healthy vocals. Because singing, the vocal cords are moving at a high rate. If the vocal cords of our voice aren't dry, they'll be more vulnerable to irritation while vibrating which can cause discomfort and pain when singing.

An effective tip for maintaining your voice is to always keep the glass of water that is lukewarm close to us every time we're singing or performing. Or, just to sip a glass of warm water prior to singing! This can help relax our vocal cords and our throat. It can also help to moisturize the muscles and tissues that are involved, which reduces the chance of damage to the vocal cords.

Habits or foods that cause problems with the voice

Consumption of these items must be lowered when singing. If we perform immediately following having consumed these foods you run the chance of damaging our vocals as well as cause unnecessary discomfort to us!

Dairy Product: Consuming a lot of dairy-based products (meat or milk, etc.)) may increase the production of mucus for some individuals, which can lead to excessive throat clearing. It is recommended to avoid dairy products prior to your singing performance because the accumulation of mucus may interfere with breathing.

Caffeinated Drinks: for serious singers, drinks with caffeine such as (coke 7up, Coke, Fanta) should be abstained from due to their potential to lead to dehydration that can make the throat, mouth as well as vocal cords dry. Acids may escape from the stomach, and then move through the esophagus and into the larynx. This can lead to the condition known as laryngopharyngeal resuscitation (or LPR. This can lead to cough and sore throat among other signs that could result in voice issues.

Gaari, chip Gaari, gaari, spicy (pepperish) food hot fried meals popcorn cigarettes, cocaine alcohol. e.t.c. These are to be avoided as much as you can.

Extreme temperatures such as hot water or cold foods cause serious damage to the voice.

The loud, shouting, or overly talking can ruin the voice.

Chapter 16: Voice Classification

(Know the Voice of yours)

The voice can be identified (soprano, alto or Tenor) once a singer is mature. It's the typical voice range that singers can use. If the singer tries to sing a different part that is difficult, it will be a challenge for the singer and does not make a pleasant sound.

Voice Parts

Both in classical and choir music, vocals are frequently defined as follows:

Bass,

Baritone,

Tenor,

Alto,

Mezzo-Soprano and

Soprano.

Tenors make up a large portion of male vocalists while many female vocalists are sopranos and altos. Treble is a misnomer by a few people, who are referring to the melodie. Everyone can sing in treble (low and high).

The type of voice is dependent on the physical dimensions and the structure of the larynx, as well as the remainder in the throat. It is a common rule that the vocal tracts have lower pitch and those who have a smaller vocal tracts are more pronounced. The physical size (e.g. the build, size) of an individual may not give a precise indicator of whether this person has a more or lower, as well as a lighter or more heavy, vocal. For determining the type of voice you have it is necessary to have an instrument that is tuned correctly for example, the guitar or keyboard, as well as an experienced individual.

A. Bass

The bass singer is thought as the lowest male member of the choirs. A common range of voice for bassists is F2-E4 and a pleasant band that typically falls between G2 to A3. (A truly bass-singing singer is not common. Actually, the majority of the choirs' bass sections consist from baritones).

b. Tenor

Tenors are thought as the best male voice. The range of a tenor is around C3 to G4, but it may be slightly different between singers.

C. Alto

The alto voice in choral music is the female voice with the lowest component, while the normal range of E3 to E5 is about.

D. Soprano

Sopranos represent the top female portion of the female voice. They typically are singing the melody for songs. Sopranos are typically likely to sing in the range C4-A5 and possibly higher. Sopranos usually have an energizing tone and typically, she has the sound of a head with a powerful voice.

Voice Range

A spectrum (number) of different notes can a vocalist's voice to sing, beginning from the note that is lowest and moving up all the way to the top note. Also, the term "range" is the difference between the top and bottom note that a performer can perform. The distance between the two notes indicates the range that a singer has. An octave range starting at C3 and end at G5 For instance is a sign that the performer can sing 2 1/2 Octaves.

Singers who aren't trained have a limited vocal range as a result of their inexperience. They aren't able to perform high notes with ease.

Natural or Normal voice (Chest register)

Chest voice is the voice that is used for speaking natural - males speak completely inside their chest register as do women who speak in both the middle and chest registers.

Head Voice

The head voice can be found just above the middle range. The phrase "head voice" is generally described as the sensation that singing's resonance occurs within the head. It is distinguished by an "ringing" tone.

Chapter 17: Extending Your Vocal Range

VOICE TRAINING EXERCISES

Every singer is able to expand their range of vocals, by doing the proper exercise routine and an instructor to help them.

StrengtheningThe Vocal Cords

A lot of singers experience the vocal cords straining and larynx swell when they sing in particular areas in their range of vocal. A strained vocal cord or excessive larynx may cause the appearance of swelling as well as other issues in the vocal cord that may be serious when singing.

The exercises we do help us perform with vocal ease and force, which is both impressive, strong and rich and yet simple.

Voice Warm-up/Exercises

It is crucial to warm the vocal chords gradually prior to beginning the strenuous performance or practice session. The vocal warm-ups can reduce strain on the voice and cause problems. Vocal folds are composed from the same type of muscle tissue that is found in other muscles of the body. The aim is to softly increase blood flow to the vocal folds to increase the responsiveness of these folds during performances.

A few examples of Voice warm-ups are:

Humming

Lip roll

Tongue screams

Neh-Neh-Neh

No-no-no

Yeah-yeah-yeah

Nuah-Nuah-Nuah

Mum-Mum-Mum

It can help you expand the range of your voice. There may be a need for a voice coach who can guide your.

Take note. When you be painful, stop. Take a break, relax and drink the fluids. Take it slow and easy. It is impossible to achieve the ideal voice in one day. Rome wasn't built in the span of a day. Keep at it, and more important, get it right.

Chapter 18: Voice Effects

The effects that are exhibited are known as Voice Dynamics. Dynamics bring life to music we sing and emphasize the words. The effects include slide, slurs, and vibratos. However, they shouldn't be utilized too often. These are decorative elements; should not put on the cake dressers before the cake is done!

The use of effects is not recommended when singing in the choir or group. This can only harm your overall performance, unless it is performing as a soloist.

Diction

The act of singing uses songs and lyrics to convey messages. If the words you use aren't precise, you're making your listeners uncomfortable as they can't discern which words you're using.

Always emphasize your consonants, k,t,p,r,b,d,.....

Make sure you open your mouth correctly to make the vowels sound a,e,i,o.

Modifying vowels to "oo" as pitches get higher. This method will allow singers to sing higher notes more easily by adjusting the vowel pronunciation. The results are quite dramatic.

Modifying vowels to "ah" as pitches get lower. This method will result in greater and more current lower notes.

Vibrato

Vibrato occurs when there is a vibrations of the diaphragm (used to breath) in order to produce slight changes in the volume or even the pitch of notes.

Vibrato is the term used by vocalists and musicians, where a sustained note can change very rapidly and in a consistent manner between a high than a lower pitch making the note feel a little shake. Vibrato refers to the sound that is a wave or pulse within the sustained note. Vibrato happens naturally and results from good breath control as well as a relaxed vocal system. Certain singers employ vibrato for expressiveness.

Ambience

This can be used to provide an atmosphere of classical singing. It involves expanding your vocal area, including your mouth and nasal space.

Loudness

'forte' means loud. 'piano' means soft. It also has many variants that lie between. Make sure you follow the cues of your instructor.

Chapter 19: Ear Training

For a musician, singer or guitarist regardless of your level, beginner or advanced, the most valuable asset you have is your ears. The art of hearing is one that's akin to a vocation. Every aspect of your music relies on the ability you have to hear. If you're looking to become the best singer you must be aware of what you can hear. When you are ready for singing, you need to imagine the note you're planning to be singing.

What is the best way to remember (score) the lyrics to a song

Make sure you know the song correctly by listening to the teacher of the song.

If the song is audio (CD or phones) then play it repeatedly and over.

Note down the lyrics and text (wordings). Take note of if it's or is in igbo or hausa language, or English the language.

It is a good idea to record songs at every the choir's practice. This can help the lyrics to stay with you.

While singing songs in memory, try to recall the way that the song is displayed on the screen.

When singing, you must always pay attention to the music that the piano is playing

How To Harmonize (part) a Song

Have you ever observed how some vocalists create harmony in a song at the very first time they listen to it, and without anyone having to show them how to do it and also without pause to study the tune? Harmony for them seems to naturally occur. When viewed from outside it could appear to be an unanswerable question: how do they decide which notes to perform when they've never ever heard of the song?

What is Harmony?

The word Harmony can describe notes which "blend" nicely with the melody. The melody is comprised of fundamental notes that make up the fundamental structure of a chorus. Harmony calls for at least two vocals or tones and may be achieved by adding any number of vocals or tones. The majority of harmony songs are written to three voice parts.

An effective way of harmonizing is to know all the tune, then

Sing it with the lower note,

Begin to sing with someone who is familiar with the tune,

Also, it helps singing on the piano

Continue to sing and harmonizing in a more independent way.

For a better understanding of harmony, play music at all times.

In the end, you'll have the ability to perform this completely by ear, but you'll need to repetition.

Notes to remember

If soprano sings melody the alto singer should be singing a little lower. Tenors need to sing less than altos.

If you're harmonizing with a singer, make sure you don't overwhelm the one who is singing the melody.

Be sure not to confuse different parts through changing. Alto and Tenor shouldn't be singing at the same time.

Find a way to be in sync with every music you listen to every day. Males can replicate certain parts of the range by with falsetto (i.e. they have a feminine voice).

If you're in the low frequency, do not try to force the issue. Lower your voice. Imagine you were telling Jim Reeves to sing like Micheal Jackson?

If you're sounding less however, you are singing exactly the same melody, then you're singing the tune. It is not a parting of anything.

You can try singing along using an MP3 player or CD player music. Make sure you pick out the right parts as you sing.

Take your time. The process of learning how to be harmonious can seem difficult for your. However, anyone can learn to achieve this feat with patience and persistence!

Take a note of yourself and listen to your recordings regularly. You'll be amazed at the way you sound.

Do not get dismayed.

Accept constructive criticism from all of your "singing teachers" without taking the criticism personally.

Try a few times before you try it publicly.

Prior to performing any form of singing, you must ensure to warm up your voice so that you don't harm the vocal chords. If you sing without warming beforehand can cause the long term damage which can lead the loss of your capacity to sing completely. The vocal chords are muscle similar to other muscle in your body. As an athlete who exercises before running to help prevent injuries and discomfort, vocalists prepare their vocals.

Treble isn't a vocal sort of. Everyone can be able to sing treble.

Diagram 1 is the most popular.

Chapter 20: Composition And Performance

How to Compose Songs

1. As composers Our main objective is to reach out to our listeners emotionally. As we develop the abilities we possess, the better we are able to write songs that have meaning.

2. Who do you write the music for? Know your audience. Complex songs can turn off people who are not the typical listener. Do not write Yoruba songs each time you go to an audience of students in a church.

3. Check out a variety of Gospel artists to see how they compare with the different styles.

4. Create a plan to write one new song each week even if it's just four lines. After you've started your track, you may include ideas in the future. This is for your mind to discover ways to explore new possibilities. The idea is to try something different each occasion.

5. The art of music is a form. Music can be used as a method to express yourself without

words. Don't become a robotic! Make your own ideas.

6. Sometimes inspiration comes unexpectedly at occasions. Write it down quickly or you could lose the idea.

7. Make use of the events through your life to be an motivation to compose music.

8. Include words in your lyrics that make your music stand out. Never compose a boring song for your listeners.

9. Do not be too serious. be a little silly around your fellow singers and musicians.

10. You can ask God for guidance. Trust Him.

PREPARING FOR MINISTRATION

Who is a Soloist?

A solo performance is not just about technique. It requires a profound knowledge of the significance of the song and the emotional dedication to express its meaning, and also receiving the backing of an ensemble. Study your lyrics and notes in sufficient detail to feel comfortable performing the song, without having to look at the text.

Then, you can begin contemplating the possible effects you can apply to the tune to give the song to life. Take a note of yourself, and then listen to it again in order to look whether you made any errors. This is a way to grow in your solo performance. Soloists who are good at their job must understand how to hear instruments, particularly the piano and drums.

Performance Presentation

First, perform the song in an intimate group, such as rehearsal, or in front of the mirror. This can help you beat stage anxiety.

The purpose of a performance is many more things than just singing. This is like preaching.

Participate in the conversation with your audience. Inspire the audience to join in.

It's much better to be at a distance than to sing nonsense. So over-practice your songs.

You should wear good clothing However, avoid bright colors or jewelry that cause distraction to your guests.

Change the stage around, avoid being rigid.

You can ask God for His grace to bless the lives of others.

Chapter 21: A To Z Singing Tips

A = Airflow. Don't hold your breath when singing. Airflow generates and transports the tone of your voice, so make sure it flows. Do not sing through your belly.

B = Breathing. Do not raise your shoulders when you take a deep breath.

C = Communicate. In the course of a performance, it's crucial to convey your message. If you commit one "mistake" don't point it at your audience. They probably didn't even know about it.

D = Dynamics. Utilizing dynamics is the process of adjusting and raising the volume of the voice to create texture and expression your voice. It is also referred to in the field of "color".

E =Emotion. If the emotion of the music you're performing can be powerful enough to affect you, allow this emotion to impact the tone of your vocals. If not, you need to reach into your soul and feel a connection with an experience similar to your individual.

F = Freedom. Do not be slave to every music genre that you like, not even your preferred one. Develop your natural and full voice, by enhancing the strength of your voice and coordination. You can then add whatever style you like.

G = Grace. If you sing, your voice will flow easily, don't force it. The volume is determined by the way of how the sound reverberates and every note will have its own "happy place".

H stands for high notes. They need constant and consistent flow of air. Students often take their breaths when they sing louder. The airflow should flow. Increase the airflow to be amazed at the results.

I = Increase. Every day, you should improve. Improve your breathing and control through breathing exercises throughout the day.

J = Jumping If have trouble getting your body fully engaged with singing, you can try some cardio exercises, such as jumping for a short time before starting once more. Sometimes, it is necessary to reenergize your voice as well as your body.

K = Know your limits. Do not sing too high or low. Do not strain or push your voice. It won't result in greater or less vocal range or stronger voice. You can destroy your voice unnecessary.

L = Larynx. It's your voice box. Be careful with it. It is the place where you can find the vocal cords. Work it out every day using honey and warm water.

M = Mirror. The practice of singing before the mirror may aid a singer in discovering many aspects of their voice. This helps to identify ways to eliminate negative habits. Make sure you use an mirror for vocal exercises however, you must be able remove the mirror and look at the audience.

N = Name. The name you use for your stage should be simple for your people watching to recall in the future. It should also be relevant to the music you perform.

O = Open your mouth. Widening your mouth will assist you in attaining a higher voice, with a more defined sound.

P = Preparation. Singers are similar to athletes. Be sure to take care of your body or instrument by stretching the vocal muscles, and releasing the body of any tension before you sing.

Q means Stop smoking. Quit speaking too loudly. Don't talk too loudly.

R = Range. If you aren't born with the range you want, but you are able to enhance it. If you're unable to reach your toes everyday to feel your toes. Eventually, it will be possible to touch your feet. It is possible to stretch your range similarly (using the correct technique) !!!) Also, if do not use all of your area often, it'll reduce.

S = Story. Singing can be like telling a story to an listeners. So why sing a song but do not relay your message? Engage yourself emotionally in the song's lyrics. Tell the story in a confident way.

T = Talent. Development without talent is a loss. It is my belief that talent is a figment of the imagination only those who have practiced for a long time will have. My students practice often, as well as those who do not - the distinction can be seen in the way they perform.

U = Uniqueness. Keep in mind that each voice has an individual fingerprint that will change with the changes in our environment, actions and health practices. Keep this in mind and take note of your voice frequently and utilize the tools for vocal training to ensure that your voice is in the best direction.

V = Vibrato. Vibrato is the spontaneous or forceful fluctuation of the singing tone. Don't focus on learning how to sing using vibrato. Instead, you should focus on the basics of breathing, singing and the support. If the right coordination is established, the vibrato can occur as it naturally.

W = Water. Water. Water. Drink water that is room temperature whenever you are able to stay well-hydrated. If you're only drinking hot or cold water at hand and you want to swish it around your mouth for a few seconds. This can prevent muscle groups from being stretched or strained by high temperatures.

Z = Zzzzzzzz. Make sure you get some sleep. If you're tired the voice you use will reflect that. An exhausted body and voice is not able to give your most authentic voice.

Chapter 22: The Diaphragm

PASSAGE OF THE BREATHING PROCESS

The breath is absorbed through it's MOUTH and the NOSE (or each). The breath travels via the PHARYNX (or neck) and is able to make a movement through the LARYNX to the TRACHEA. It is also known as the windpipe. is connected to the larynx inside the neck, to the Thorax. It is divided into two BRONCHI and then enters the lungs and then branches which then divide into smaller tubes that end within air sacs of the LUNGS. The heart and the lungs are a part of the Thoracic space. The right lung is comprised of three lobes: an upper and middle lobe, as well as a lower. The left lung has an upper as well as lower. The lungs are cylindrical in form and are shaped to follow the contours of the interior of the chest. If the chest gets larger, the lungs take on a form.

THE ORDER OF THE BREATHING PROCESS

The purpose of breathing is to supply oxygen to blood. If the quantity of carbon dioxide within the blood stream is at some level of tension, breathing muscles get stimulated to start contraction.

The muscles contract and expand the chest area.

The air that is breathed into airways, which equalizes the pressure of the oxygen in the lungs as well as the air outside.

The muscles stop contracting while the chest reverts to its size.

The breath is released when the volume of the lungs decreases, thereby equilibrating the pressure that exists between the air inside the lungs as well as the air outside.

When breathing with ease, around one-tenth of the volume of air inside the lungs moves between the lungs. This is referred to as TIDAL Air. The volume of tidal air will increase significantly in the blink of an eye, but more than 50% of the air is retained in the lungs. This is referred to as RESIDUAL air. A quarter of it remains when you blow out your lungs with a lot of force.

THE FIRST STEP AND THE MOST KEY ELEMENT IN IMPROVING, ENRICHING AND PURIFYING SOUND IS TO LEARN THE ART OF DIAPHRAGMATIC BREATHING.

FIRST READ THE FOLLOWING OUTLOUD, PREFERABLY RECORDING YOUR SOUND. THEN FOLLOW THE SECTION ON DIAPHRAGMATIC BREATHING AND TRY AGAIN.

WARM-UP EXERCISES

On the rock, the wild rascal sprinted.

Sea-shells are sold on the beach

John and Jinni enjoyed yellow Jell O mixed with juice and jam.

Although there was thought to be three people, it was actually 33 for tea.

Fergal prepared a fish fry for his pals on Fridays.

Lillian was a fan of learning languages such as Latin.

TIP - FOR PUREST SOUND PRACTISE THE ABOVE WITH A PENCIL OR STRAW HELD BETWEEN YOUR LIPS. THIS WILL BRING THE VOICE FORWARDS AND HELP YOU TO PROJECT.

FOR ACCENTS, PRACTISE SPEAKING IN A WHISPER AND THEN GRADUALLY INCREASING SOUND. GO BACK TO A WHISPER WHENEVER THE ACCENT PREVAILS.

Under Milk Wood - Dylan Thomas

Beginning at the start.

It is spring, moonless night in the small town, starless and bible-black, the cobble streets silent and the hunched, courters'-and-rabbits' wood limping invisible down to the sloe black, slow, black, crow black, fishing boat-bobbing sea. The homes are as dark like moles (though moles can see clearly this evening in the snouting velvet buzzes) or blind like captains. Cat with the hushed central area by the pump and the clock of the town, the stores in mourning, in mourning, the Welfare Hall in widows' the weeds. The people of the sleepy and confused town, are now asleep.

How do we get anxious?

Certain life circumstances can cause stress. However, everyday events can create anxiety or overwhelmed, possibly often.

There are people who get anxious when deadlines must be met or if they're running late to an appointment. It is normal to feel anxious when there are congestion! Meeting certain people could cause us to feel less comfortable.

Do a quick note the situations that you believe could cause you to become anxious. If you become aware of these scenarios, you'll be better equipped to manage the tension that may arise.

What are we able to do about tension?

TENSION IN THE NECK AND SHOULDERS WILL AFFECT BOTH YOUR BREATHING AND YOUR SOUND. THIS CAN HAVE A SERIOUS AFFECT ON THE QUALITY OF YOUR VOICE. FIRST WORK TO CREATE A MORE RELAXED POSTURE. THIS WILL HELP YOU IN OTHER ASPECTS OF YOUR LIFE TOO.

When you recognize indications of tension within yourself and identify which times you're likely to feel stressed then you are able to work towards getting more comfortable.

There are many methods to assist yourself. It is possible to try a an assortment of exercises or actions.

Relaxation techniques - yoga and meditation, as well as hypnosis, Some can be done at home, while others require the assistance of a teacher. Relaxing Activities

Saunas and hot baths Massage, bathing, listening to music, reading or music, palate exercises, stretching. Avoid overexerting in one of them, even when you are doing them for relaxation, or else you'll defeat your goal of doing the exercise.

Chapter 23: Diaphragmatic Breathing

The breathing technique of the diaphragm should be practiced regularly. Begin with a minimum of three minutes before increasing to approximately 30 seconds per every day. Once you've completed 10 minutes and you will notice that you breathe normally and comfortably from your diaphragm. This habit will become the normal way of breathing.

Benefits of breathing diaphragmatically is not limited to just voice. Your vocal tone, resonance, and tone will increase, it will also allow you to increase your endurance and discover that it can aid in reducing stress as well as positively affect your overall wellbeing too.

Exercise

Begin with shaking your hands until you reach the floor and loosening the tension in your shoulder, wrists and hands.

Make your mouth open and sound the word OH which is the same as a word.

It's almost like a monkey. Repeat the sound of OH repeatedly while shaking your hands on the floor.

Move forward and reach the floor, if you are able for every OH sound, breath as you lift your body.

Practice this routine each day. If you are unsure about whether or not you're doing your diaphragm correctly, lay your hands over the diaphragm and feel the sound.

TIP COPY THE PAGES YOU USE DAILY ONTO CARD OR PASTE THEM ONTO CARD. YOU CAN THEN HOLD THEM EASILY WHEN WORKING.

When an exercise is completed properly, there will not be any hyperventilation or shortness of breath. After it is become habitual breathing will flow naturally and effortlessly and continue to flow throughout the day.

You shouldn't expect to accomplish this in a matter of minutes. It has been a habit to breathe through your stomach and ribcage throughout your entire life. Just like any new practice, you will need to work on it to get the new habit established.

VOCAL CARE

This is a simple instruction on maintaining your voice healthy.

DO NOT SMOKE.

DO NOT STRAIN YOUR VOICE.

Do not speak in opposition to background sounds. Television, Radio and washing machines, etc.

Do not shout in order to draw anyone's attention.

Don't drink sharp spirits because they make your throat feel dry.

Don't cough in order to clean your throat. Instead, try drinking or swallowing drinking water.

Be careful not to strain your voice whether you are singing or talking. Warm-up first.

Do not chew menthol or sweets made of glycerine to ease your throat since they could cause irritation.

Don't eat at night. the night.

Don't cough in order to figure whether your voice is correct. Hum instead.

Increase the humidity of your house.

DO talk in a relaxed and relaxed manner.

Do take note of this if you often use your voice in your work.

Do drink lots of water.

Make sure to take a break from your voice when you use the voice for a long time.

DO make use of steam inhalation to treat colds.

Stretch, warm up and apply relaxation techniques to boost your confidence as well as vocal projection.

WARM-UP STRETCHES

Begin by doing some yoga exercises and then the yawning. Bring your arms towards the ceiling, then lower them down towards the floor and reach your toes. Release any tension from your wrists, hands, and fingers. Move your body back into alignment.

Practice one of the techniques for relaxation mentioned earlier.

Take a deep breath slowly and slow by chanting 'SH', if you enjoy it. Stop - let breath to enter slowly and effortlessly.

Inhale slowly and exhale slowly by breathing through the nostrils and out through your mouth multiple times.

Proper posture is crucial. Keep your weight evenly on both feet, and giving a small amount of movement to the knees' back. The body should be at ease and your shoulders slightly towards the back, and your eyes directly ahead, and your chin firmly held however not being pushed forward. It is possible to centralize your posture by keeping your eyes on an object that is in alignment to your own line of sight.

Take a couple of minutes to chew to loosen any tension from the jaw. Perform neck and shoulder relaxation exercises. You can also roll your over the neck from side to side or around and in a round.

Fix your face with a screw and then ease it back to ensure that your muscles are calm before starting vocal exercises.

PRACTISE EXERCISE TO BE USED IN YOUR DAILY WORK.

TIP - MASTER THE MORE SIMPLE EXERCISES FIRST. USE THE FOLLOWING ONLY WHEN YOU ARE CONFIDENT AND COMPETENT AND HAVE ESTABLISHED A SOUND THAT YOU ARE SATISFIED WITH.

POETRY READING

Message - Wendy Cope

Make sure you pick up the phone before it's already too late.

and dial my phone number. You'll have no time leftand I'm waiting to hear from you.

Already, love is turning into the hate

Very soon, I'll begin to search for alternatives.

Men of the past like yours are very rare.

If you want to know me at an cost

This is guaranteed to send me mad.

Make sure you pick up the phone before it's too to late.

Well. It would be great to consume

Our relationship while we've had hair and teeth?

Remember that you're 38 years old.

and dial my phone number. You've got no time left.

Is there a new love affair with kamikaze?

No chance. The next time, I'll need learn how to be patient

However, one day more is way more than I could take I'm not able to bear it.

The love is already changing to hate.

My friends claim that I am exaggerating.

Also, they often dramatize. It's reasonable

It's not pleasure to be in this state.

Very soon, I'll begin looking elsewhere.

I'm sure that you're fond of me, however I would never dare

You can call me again. Instead, I'll be concentrating

Sending thought-waves across the London air

If they do reach you, do not hesitate and don't hesitate to respond

Answer the phone.

Giving Up Smoking

There's no Shakespeare sonnet.

Or a Beethoven quartet

It's much easier to love than it is to like

It is also more difficult to remember.

Do you think it seems like a lot?

I'm still not done -

I love you more than I'd want to

Smoking cigarettes.

Chapter 24: Breath And Sound

Breathe in slowly - stop - let loose tension wide mouth - breathe inthen pause and wait until you are able to breathe back inbreathe to come in, and continue to breathe in.

Similar to above, but with a sigh out for ten count silently.

Like the previous example, but you'll be you're humming for 10 counts and making as loud as you are able to.

Like above, singing on vowel sounds like oo Oo, Aw, Ah Ay, Ee, each time for 10 counts. Resonance is felt throughout the body.

Repeat steps 1-4 until you have 15 total.

Connecting Breath and Sound

Shoulders raise an inch and release, and then a deeper release of shoulders.

Drop your head, feel the muscles lifting the head back to an the upright position. Bring your chin into.

Drop of the head sideways and then head roll.

Smile gently and move your head inwards.

The hand is placed on the stomach just below the waist. Then, fill it up and release the breath onto V as well as Z.

Make contact with Ah three times and feel air slow down and then start to make the sound. Continue singing on vowel.

PROBLEM WORDS

BLACK TAP HAT

STACK KNACK RACK

NOW KNOW HOW

ALTHOUGH ROW SEW

THAT FLAT MAT SAT THROUGH BLEW

ENOUGH ROUGH RAW DOOR FLOOR ROAR

SIMPLE SAMPLE RAMP AMPLE TIRED WERE

THING BRING YOUNG WINGS YOUR THIS

WONDER WANDER UNDER SING SONG SANG

UP CUP PARCEL CAT AFTER YAWN

BROWN DOWN YELL YELLOW THEM THEY

THOSE KIND GOING OWING OUR HOUR

The following is a listing of words that are frequently mispronounced. It can assist in resolving issues with speaking, like consonant 'S' or recusant "R". Additionally, it can help to correct slow speech issues when you use it often as part of a exercises for improving your voice.

NASAL SPEECH - IF YOUR SPEECH IS NASAL OR YOU HAVE AN ACCENT SUCH AS LIVERPOOL, BIRMINGHAM OR ANOTHER NORTHERN REGION, YOU SHOULD PRACTICE THE ABOVE WITH A PENCIL IN YOUR MOUTH, SO THAT YOU ARE FORCED TO PROJECT YOUR VOICE FORWARDS.

THIS IS ALSO A USEFUL TECHNIQUE FOR IMPROVING THE QUALITY OF YOUR SPEECH

AND BUILDING A BBC ENGLISH, OR RECEIVED PRONUNCIATION SOUND.

ORGANS OF SPEECH

Once you have established a proper breathing stream that allows the voice will flow and out, the organs that are active include tongue, lips, teeth, and the soft palate. The jaw's lower part is required to be open and relaxed.

For even greater results. When you've master these steps, you can proceed to enhancing the organs of speech.

EXERCISES FOR THE ORGANS OF SPEECH

JAW. Lower jaw should be dropped open until it hangs at a comfortable angle with its jaw wide open. The jaw should be opened and closed repeatedly and with different rates. Say ah-ss-ah four times slowly. Repeat four times more quickly. YAWN.

TONGUE-TIP & HARD PALATE. The mouth should be wide open. While making sure it is wide-open, position the tip of your tongue between the upper teeth. Then, behind lower teeth. Repeat slow and 4 times. Repeat four times more quickly. The tongue should be directed to various parts of your mouth. Say lah-lah-lah three times increasing speed.

BACK OF TONGUE & SOFT PALATE. Widen your mouth, keep the tongue's tip flat. lift back tongue, to flatten multiple times. Say ah-ng-ah-hg-ah-ng-ah. Speak k and g many times while keeping your jaw wide.

TEETH. Train upper and the lower one with repetitions of V, F repeatedly. Practice the tongue and teeth using TH repetition in the similar manner.

LIPS. Practice forward lip postures such as oo, ah Oo. Repeated repeatedly. Create words using these positions What is your name? Or oo, oh, ah. It's a long way to go!

Practise patter exercises. I.e.

In a quiet, solemn slumber on a dark and dull dock

In a septic prison, with an all-life lock

In anticipation of the feeling of a brief sharp shock

From a cheap, chippy cutter on a huge black block.

(Gilbert and Sullivan)

EXERCISES FOR VOICE PRODUCTION

PRACTICE THE FOLLOWING WAYS OF SIGHING

Sigh, voiceless

- In a voice

It's easy and relaxing without any strain or constriction of the throat.

A yawn can release tension from jaw and face.

It encourages a yawning/sighing and a relaxing of the vocal tract, and allows for easy airflow. It reduces the size of the larynx (voice box) making it simpler to make a great voice.

Relax and breathe through your mouth, breathe in, hold and then breathe it out with your nostrils.

Check to see if you're using the proper pitch to your hum, and it is a good idea to raise and lower the pitch. It should be possible to change the pitch of the note with no difficulties.

Chapter 25: Counting, The Breathy Approach

Counting In Groups of Numbers

When you've found the perfect pitch and breathy sound and you are able to keep it, breath between every group of numbers. 123, 456, 789.

The Breathy Approach -(Marilyn Monroe)

You should allow more air to flow over your vocal cords like you're trying to draw more oxygen in after you've run.

HOO HA

HOH HAY

HAH HEE

Learn to spell words with H

HAT HIGH

HEAT HAND

HIT HUNG

Learn short sentences. Practice reading aloud, 4 word sentences per paragraph, then longer sentences and paragraphs. Then conversations.

Soon you'll be able to have your voice to match the screen and stage. Develop your breathing control, projection and durability. Work your vocal cords the same way as you would do any other body part and it will benefit you.

VOICE EXERCISES

Tongue Twisters (Repeat at a faster speed and then faster)

Leather in yellow, red.

The yellow and red lorries.

Mixed Biscuits.

Unique New York

Richard handed Robin his ribs after he roasted his rabbit which is a uncommonly.

Sly Sam takes a sip of Sally's soup.

Betty purchased a small amount of butter.

The butter Betty bought tasted very bitter.

Then Betty got a larger amount of butter.

The butter that Betty purchased before.

Six swans with sleek bodies swam quickly towards the south.

In the event that a gumboil boils oil,

What is the amount of oil that make a boil of gumboil?

Gumboils can boil oil.

Three gray geese on a grassy field,

Grey was the color of geese, and green was for grasing.

How much wood will the chuck of a woodchuck contain?

What if a woodchuck was able to be able to chuck wood?

These exercises offer a perfect speech warm-up. It helps you concentrate your attention and loosening the jaw and tongue to prepare for the next vocal exercises.

SOFT PALATE

A muscle that is located behind of the tongue's roof. The muscle opens and closes opening towards the mouth.

After yawning say...

OOK OHK AWK AHK AYK

EEK OOG OHG AWG AHG AYG EEG

OONG OHNG AWNG AHNG AYNG EENG

You can you can feel your soft palate expanding.

Poetry practice

On the Ning Nang Nong

In which cows they bong!

All the monkeys say"BOO!"

There's a Nong Nang Ning

Where do the trees go to ping!

Teapots and teapots go jibber Joo.

On the Nong Ning Nang

The mice all go bang!

It's impossible to catch these guys when they are!

So it's Ning Nang Nong!

Cows go bong!

Nong Nang Ning!

Trees go ping!

Nong Ning Nang!

Mice squeak!

It's a raucous place to be a part of

Is the Ning Nang Ning Nang Nong!

TECHNIQUE

An effective voice is achievable through regular practice and becoming conscious of how you sound throughout your speaking. Be aware of weaknesses and make the effort to fix the issues. Speech is first learned through imitation, and the more attentive we are to the correct pronunciation of speaking, the greater can imitate it. It's important to pay attention to people who can speak clearly, i.e. BBC radio presenters and newscasters that, in general have been selected for their excellent speaking voice.

www.ingramcontent.com/pod-product-compliance
Lightning Source LLC
Chambersburg PA
CBHW071341120626
46546CB00002B/652